Academic Literacy in the English Classroom

Helping Underprepared and Working Class Students Succeed in College

EDITED BY
Carolyn R. Boiarsky

Boynton/Cook Publishers
HEINEMANN
Portsmouth, NH

Boynton/Cook Publishers, Inc.
A subsidiary of Reed Elsevier Inc.
361 Hanover Street
Portsmouth, NH 03801–3912
www.boyntoncook.com

Offices and agents throughout the world

The editor and publisher wish to thank those who have generously given permission to reprint borrowed material:

"Digging" from *Opened Ground: Selected Poems: 1966–1996* by Seamus Heaney. Copyright © 1998 by Seamus Heaney. Reprinted by permission of Farrar, Straus and Giroux, LLC, New York, and Faber and Faber Ltd., London.

"Mapmaking" from *Mapmaker Revisited* by Beatriz Badikian. Copyright © 1999 by Beatriz Badikian. Published by Gladsome Books, Chicago. Reprinted by permission of the poet.

Library of Congress Cataloging-in-Publication Data
Academic literacy in the English classroom : helping underprepared and working class students succeed in college / edited by Carolyn R. Boiarsky.
    p. cm.
Includes bibliographical references.
  ISBN 0-86709-525-3
  1. Language arts (Secondary). 2. College preparation programs.
  3. Academic achievement. 4. Working class—Education (Secondary).
I. Boiarsky, Carolyn R.

LB1631.A343 2003
428'.0071'2—dc21   2003005425

Editor: Lisa Luedeke
Production service: The GTS Companies/York, PA Campus
Production coordinator: Elizabeth Valway
Cover design: Suzanne Heiser, Night & Day Design
Manufacturing: Steve Bernier

Printed in the United States of America on acid-free paper
07 06 05 04 03 VP 1 2 3 4 5

To Clement Stacy with whom I spent many a lively evening engaged in hot debate over the various issues raised in this book and whose incisive questioning led me to question my own stance, to search deeper for answers, to expand my horizons, and often to arrive at new truths.

Contents

Acknowledgments

I want to thank Peter Stillman, who supported this book from its inception, and Lisa Ludeke, who recognized it as a valuable addition to the many texts Boynton/Cook has published to help teachers prepare students to succeed in whatever they choose to do, whether it be to continue in their education or to enter the workplace. I would also like to thank my working-class grandfather, a postal carrier, who, when I was growing up, would periodically stop at the "dead letter office" after he had walked his route to collect the children's magazines that were there and bring them home for me to read.

And, then, I need to thank three colleagues, David Pick who read through one of my chapters to make certain my adaptations of cognitive psychology were appropriate, and Michael Dobberstein who helped me phrase my explorations of cognitive psychology clearly & elegantly. And finally Robert Selig who found the exquisite quote on p. 80 for me.

—Carolyn Boiarsky

Introduction

We would gather late Tuesday nights in Julie's office after teaching our classes, our adrenaline still running high, and I would listen as Judith and Julie talked about their developmental courses, their frustrations and victories. Small victories, but won nevertheless. A thought-provoking question asked, a sudden recognition of how to express something, a slow dawning that there are connections among ideas. At that time of night, classes are filled mainly with nontraditional students: women tired of raising children, men trying to get out of the steel mills, men and women wanting to know more than what they hadn't learned in high school, trying to master the rudiments of reading and writing that would allow them to enter the academy. I listened as Judith and Julie talked about teaching annotation, syntax structures, and strategies for reading and writing, strategies I took for granted that students who arrived in college—and in high school for that matter—already knew. I listened as they described their students' attitudes—not wanting to spend the time to reread a section of a book or to go through the revision process for a paper, not thinking of reading a good book or a poem as a pleasurable activity, never perceiving themselves acquiring knowledge to make knowledge, or recognizing school as anything more than a way to get a job. I recognized the same lack of skills, the same attitudes in many of my technical writing students.

It was on one of these nights, sipping tea that Julie had brewed in the small white china teapot she kept in her office, that this book was born. It would be a book about first-generation college students from working-class backgrounds and immigrant families. It would be a book in which the authors would tell others what they had learned that might help them prepare their students for joining the academic conversation. I hoped it might be a book that could preempt the problems the present students faced.

The book expanded. Beyond Purdue, beyond the Midwest. Kelly Belanger, who had moved from Youngstown University to the University of Wyoming, and Diane Panozzo, who taught at a nearby high school in Cheyenne, teamed up to write a chapter. Closer to the initiators, Steve Fox, who taught at IU-PUI (Indiana University-Purdue University Indianapolis) wrote an essay.

These authors represent a wide range of backgrounds. Julie comes from a rural farm family in Iowa; Judith grew up in a minister's household and lived in small towns along the eastern seaboard from Florida to New Jersey; while Carolyn and Steve grew up in professional families, Carolyn in the suburbs of

Philadelphia and Steve in Wisconsin. Most of the authors, too, have had lives outside the academy. Carolyn worked as a reporter for UPI, Steve and Judith as high school teachers, and Julie as a librarian. They also represent a range of ages, from 40 to 60, and a range of Ph.D. generations, from the early 1980s to the late 1990s.

All of these authors write from their own experiences, their own perspectives. Yet they all focus on similar ideas, stress similar knowledges and attitudes, perceive their students in similar ways, and question some of the same presentday trends. They all use a process approach to teaching and perceive, as their end goals, the empowerment of their students as informed citizens. They believe that, regardless of whether their students are children of the working class or the middle or professional classes, or whether they are ESL students or American-born native speakers, they need to acquire academic literacy if they are to succeed in the academy. And they all recognize that, to prepare students to enter the academy, their classrooms need to be both humane and challenging, that by the time students enter their senior year in high school much of the scaffolding that has been constructed since the elementary grades needs to be removed so that the students can begin to learn on their own. In trying to distinguish students by class, the authors also seem to arrive at similar conclusions, finding that working-class students have the same needs as most students. In fact, all of the authors struggle to define working class as distinct from middle or professional class. In an effort to solve this dilemma, Julie suggests that rather than categorize students by class, we should categorize them according to whether or not they have acquired academic literacy. For those who have not, she adopts the term "underprepared." Finally Steve questions whether he should teach to class at all.

Thus, while this book first began with the authors looking specifically at working-class students, in its final version the book is concerned with all students who have not acquired academic literacy. It is written on the assumption that students are going to be expected to read textbooks written in traditional technical, jargon-laden style; write research papers using appropriate field-specific language and conventions; and discuss topics in the form appropriate for the respective fields; and that we need to prepare students to accomplish these tasks.

However, the book's focus is not on content knowledge. For years the discipline has battled over whether students should have depth or breadth, whether they should know the traditional canon or the "new" canon, or if there is a canon at all. The answer is "yes" to all of the above. They need depth. They also need breadth. They should know some Shakespeare, *Huckleberry Finn.* They should also know *The Bluest Eye.* They should know the poetry of the Odyssey, Wordsworth and Keats and Maya Angelou, the novels of George Eliot and Ernest Hemingway and Sandra Cisneros, the essays of Jonathan Swift and James Baldwin and Joan Didion and William Least Heat Moon. How to pile it all into forty-minute periods over ten months for four years seems an impossible task. It is. Unless students read on their own, during summers, during vacations, during dull periods on their jobs, they will never be able to cover all of the literature that they will study in more depth in college. For these reasons, this book does not attempt to provide an answer to the content question. Rather than consider specific literary works and discourse genres, the authors discuss the strategies students need to acquire if they are to understand and write a critical analysis of an excerpt from Plato, or an essay by Richard Rodriguez, or a short story by Amy Tan when they are assigned to read them in a literature or composition class.

Academic Literacy in the English classroom is composed of eight chapters. Chapter 1 examines one of the underlying concepts of this book—that working-class students have special needs in the academy. It provides a brief history of the working class in American institutions of higher education and then examines present-day perceptions of working-class characteristics as they affect student success in the academy. Chapter 2 is concerned with general cognitive strategies that students need in order to transfer information and to learn to learn. It discusses the strategies involved in information transfer and provides a variety of methods and activities for helping students acquire process and contextual knowledge related to these strategies. Chapters 3 through 8 concentrate on domain-specific strategies. Boiarsky in Chapter 3, Fox in Chapter 4, and Belanger and Panozzo in Chapter 5 discuss strategies for writing. Burdan offers strategies for reading in general in Chapter 6 and for reading literature specifically in Chapter 7. In Chapter 8, Hagemann discusses the language of the academy and its relation specifically to students with nonstandard American English dialects and to students for whom English is their second language.

As you read, you will note that the authors' approaches to teaching diverge to some degree. Boiarsky seems more structured than Belanger, Panozzo, and Fox; while Hagemann, and Burdan appear willing to leave more scaffolding standing than Boiarsky, Belanger, and Panozzo. We have not attempted to reconcile these differences. Instead, we leave it to you, our readers, to enter into a conversation with us as you consider our various approaches in the following chapters and decide for yourselves those that meet your present needs.

—Carolyn Boiarsky

1

Working-Class Students in the Academy

Who Are They?

Carolyn Boiarsky with Julie Hagemann and Judith Burdan

Between my finger and my thumb
The squat pen rests.

Under my window, a clean rasping sound
When the spade sinks into gravelly ground:
My father digging. I look down

Till his straining rump among the flower beds
Bends low, comes up twenty years away
Stooping in rhythm through potato drills
Where he was digging.

The coarse boot nestled on the lug, the shaft
Against the inside knee was levered firmly.
He rooted out tall tops, buried the bright edge deep
To scatter new potatoes that we picked
Loving their cool hardness in our hands.

By God, the old man could handle a spade.
Just like his old man.

My grandfather cut more turf in a day
Than any other man on Toner's bog.
Once I carried him milk in a bottle
Corked sloppily with paper. He straightened up
To drink it, then fell to right away
Nicking and slicing neatly, heaving sods
Over his shoulder, going down and down for the
good turf. Digging.

The cold smell of potato mould, the squelch and slap
Of soggy peat, the curt cuts of an edge
Through living roots awaken in my head.
But I've no spade to follow men like them.

Between my finger and my thumb
The squat pen rests.
I'll dig with it.

—Seamus Heaney

Most of the students I teach at Purdue University Calumet in Hammond, Indiana, an industrial suburb of Chicago, come from working-class families. They are very similar to the students I used to teach at the Community College in the heartland of the Midwest, Peoria, Illinois, and, except for their dialect, do not differ markedly from my students in rural Sissonville, West Virginia. Most are first-generation college students, and most of their parents hold blue-collar or low-level service jobs. Even those whose parents are in managerial or entrepreneurial positions work in manufacturing or construction, traditionally considered working-class occupations. Their offices are not in the sun-reflecting glass and steel skyscrapers of downtown Chicago but in the Dickensian dark brown and red brick plants of the 1920s, 1930s, and 1940s, surrounded by grey smoke-billowing steel plants and oil refineries on the south side of the city. Some of these students are immigrants, having arrived from Greece and Mexico; others have relocated from Puerto Rico. Others were born in America but are growing up in homes where their parents still speak Polish, Spanish, or Serbian, the language of the country from which they emigrated. Some of them come from small towns to the south, farm towns, where their parents work in small shops as mechanics, salespersons, clerks, nurses aides. Most of the students themselves work. They have jobs doing inventory in supermarkets, keeping the books for a steel-rolling plant, logging in merchandise for a warehouse discount store, maintaining a machine at one of the steel mills. Some have no difficulty adjusting to college life; others find themselves lost, unable to figure out what they're supposed to do, what it takes to succeed. It is these latter ones who struggle in freshman composition and introductory literature classes.

This chapter establishes a framework for understanding the background and characteristics of students from working-class families and the need for providing these students with academic literacy so that they can succeed in college English. The remainder of this book discusses various methods and strategies to help these students in their first-year composition and literature classes.

Historical Background

For college to become a possibility for the majority of working-class Americans, three criteria must be met: (1) a relevant curriculum, (2) sufficient funding, and (3) easy access. From the inception of this nation, there has been a growing movement to make universities accessible, both geographically and financially, to the working class and to expand the curriculum to encompass their interests and needs by providing them with an education that combines the theoretical with the practical/vocational, the classical with the technical/scientific. The establishment of a variety of institutions—metropolitan, land grant, state, junior, and community colleges—and the passage of two major legislative acts—the Morrill Act and the GI Bill—along with special financial arrangements over the past 250 years have provided working-class students with a growing number of opportunities in higher education. Today, with an increasing number of institutions with open admissions policies, coupled with government loans and the advent of distance education via the Internet, college has become accessible to just about anyone who wishes to attend.

Until the middle of the nineteenth century, universities were mainly the prerogative of the wealthy and of those who wanted to enter the ministry. Even among those who were wealthy, many did not choose to attend institutions of higher education, as there was no real need. Universities provided a strictly liberal education with studies centering in the classics: Latin and Greek literary works, Greek philosophy, logic, metaphysics, and rhetoric (Schmidt, 1962). If students wanted to pursue careers related to surveying or accounting, they apprenticed themselves to someone already in the trade—they didn't go to a university.

However, there were exceptions to the classic university model. Rather than perceiving higher education as the milieu for a small intellectual elite, some of the early colonial leaders recognized that a college education was needed if there was to be an educated citizenry. Thomas Jefferson, who founded the University of Virginia in 1825, expounded, "If a nation expects to be ignorant and free in a state of civilization it expects what never was and never will be" (cited in Callahan, 1957, p. 125). These leaders also understood that scientific knowledge for both agriculture and industry was necessary for the country's continued economic growth. As early as 1749, Benjamin Franklin, in a pamphlet entitled "Proposals for the Education of Youth in Pensilvania [sic]" proposed an "academy" to teach "Everything that is useful and everything that is ornamental." Franklin's academy became the College of Philadelphia and later the University of Pennsylvania. It was the first secular college in America, and it attracted a broader segment of the population than the church schools of Harvard, Yale, and William and Mary (Penn Web Steering Committee, 2002).

With the advent of Jacksonian democracy, the idea of the secular university gained prominence with "special interest" colleges springing up to reflect the various religions, genders, ethnic backgrounds, and geographic locales of a changing American society. But while these institutions provided a higher education for an expanding and changing population, they mainly continued to offer a classical curriculum, and only those who could afford both the time and the cost attended. The only working-class students who enrolled in these colleges were those identified for their special talents and sent to school on scholarship (Jencks and Reisman, 1977).

Thus, instruction in the sciences and technology for members of the population who would be involved in these areas fell to the responsibility of the state legislatures and the federal government. As America emerged from the colonial period and began to develop its industries as well as an agricultural economy based on mechanization and new scientific knowledge, state legislatures recognized that the traditional college did not provide an education in terms of a scientific, practical curriculum and therefore did not serve the members of most communities. To correct this situation, they began to assume responsibility for the higher education of their citizenry. The University of Virginia was the first of these[1] (Hofstadter and Smith, 1961).

The federal government also recognized the need for all of its citizens to be educated to understand their responsibility in a democracy as well as to help the economy grow by adding their knowledge to the country's industrial and agricultural base. The Northwest Ordinance, passed in 1787, required the new states of Ohio, Michigan, Wisconsin, Illinois, and Indiana to set aside land for institutions of higher education. The Ordinance set the pattern for the Morrill Act, passed in 1862, which required all of the states to set land aside for institutions of higher education that would provide instruction in "such branches of learning as are related to agriculture and the mechanic arts...in order to promote the liberal and practical education of the industrial classes in the several pursuits and professions of life..." (Hofstadter and Smith, 1961, p. 568). The institutions resulting from this Act became known as the "Land-Grant Colleges."

The Morrill Act extended the idea of higher education for the "industrial" class past the Appalachians to the states on the eastern seaboard. The most prominent of the institutions established under this Act in the east was Cornell University, where the two founders, Ezra Cornell and Andrew Dickson, declared it was to be a place where "anyone could learn anything" (Brickman and Lehrer, 1962, p. 74). With the establishment of land-grant colleges, universities began to take on the role of job training (Callahan, 1957). In his 1908 commencement address at the University of Wisconsin, Lord James Bryce, the British Ambassador to the United States, stated, "Whereas the universities of Germany...have been popular but not free, and those of England free but not popular, yours...are both popular and free....Nor is it only that your universities are accessible to all classes. They have achieved what has never been achieved before—they have led all classes of the people to believe in the value of university education and wish to attain it. They have made it seem a necessary part of the equipment of everyone who can afford the time to take it" (Brickman and Lehrer, 1962, pp. 78–9).

The Civil War became a turning point in universities' democratization and marked the turning point for universities' recognition of the need to provide for the working class. Following the war, two trends—a growing manufacturing base in the cities and the beginning of agribusiness in the rural areas of the country, brought about by the use of scientific methods for improving crops on the farms and plantations—reinforced the need for universities to provide vocational and scientific training to all citizens. "American civilization generated an almost irresistible drive for the popularization of opportunities for learning, and one of the most notable aspects of this movement was a constant increase in the percentage of the population enjoying the benefits of a higher education" (Brickman and Lehrer 1962, p. 24).

Since the end of the nineteenth century, higher education in America has been intertwined with the education of the working class. Various permutations of postsecondary institutions have developed to meet the needs of an ever-expanding population base. At the same time that land-grant colleges were springing up in the rural sections of the country, metropolitan universities such as City College of New York (CCNY) and Temple University in Philadelphia were being established to provide for working-class students living in cities. The movement was spurred by an influx of working-class immigrants to eastern cities. Unlike the residence campuses of Harvard, Yale, and Penn, where classes were conducted during the day and students spent most of their free time engaged in clubs, fraternity events, and such sporting activities as sculling and dueling, classes at these urban institutions were held at night so students could hold jobs during the day. By the early twentieth century these institutions had relocated to areas served by public transportation, providing students with easy access to them. In fact, they were often referred to as "subway schools."

The City College of New York was first established as the Free Academy for the education of children of the working class and immigrants. Townsend Harris, the force behind the college, believed not only that the masses should have an opportunity to acquire a postsecondary education but also that it was necessary for that education to be free. The Free Academy Act was passed by the New York legislature in 1847, and the Academy opened its doors two years later, offering a combination of studies that included the classical subjects of Greek, Latin, and moral and intellectual philosophy, along with such scientific studies as physics and chemistry and such career-oriented training as bookkeeping, civil engineering, and stenography (DeCicco, 1997).

Temple University was established when a young man approached Russell Conwell, a prominent lawyer and journalist in Philadelphia, and asked if there was a way he could receive training to become a minister. The prospective student had found that because he worked during the day, he couldn't attend classes at any of the local colleges. Conwell agreed to teach him in the evening. When the time arrived for the first class, the new student appeared with six others, all in the same predicament that he was in. As word of the night school spread, more and more students, who recognized it as an opportunity to acquire an education, began attending. In 1888, Conwell obtained a charter for "The Temple College" that, significantly, selected the owl as its mascot. The university, like CCNY, has provided thousands upon thousands of working-class students with opportunities to attend college during the evening after they have finished working. Many a man, like my father during the early part of the twentieth century, worked all day, then attended classes at night and in-between courted the woman who would eventually become his wife. My father would sleep in the subway on the way home from my mother's house.

Although the various legislative acts along with the growth in state, land-grant, and metropolitan colleges provided opportunities for working-class students, only a small percentage were able to take advantage of them. Except at CCNY, these colleges, including the state and land-grant universities, were forced to charge students, as the state allocations were not sufficient to cover their costs. Although tuition was lower than that at private universities, the tuition still created an economic hardship for many who were coming from families that were not living far above the poverty line. Further-more, there remained little incentive for members of the working class to go to college, as many jobs did not require college degrees. It was not until the passage of the GI Bill in 1944 that the members of the working class entered the nation's colleges in large numbers. For the first time, monies went to the students rather than to the institutions, giving the GIs the funds they needed both to support themselves and to pay the cost of tuition. Bennett (2000) suggests that it is the passage of this bill that "made a reality of Jefferson's concept of creating independent yeoman." It is estimated that more than 2 million veterans attended college under the GI Bill. In 1947, forty-nine percent of all students were veterans. The GI Bill not only provided World War II veterans with the financial ability to attend college but it also provided them with a stimulus for doing so. Worried about employment problems caused by the huge influx of returning GIs, the federal government encouraged them to use their benefits to attend local colleges (Stacy and Dobberstein, 1999).

With the GI Bill enabling so many people to attend college, the number of junior colleges increased, providing the GIs with a variety of alternatives for higher education. Although junior colleges had been in existence since the early part of the twentieth century, most simply offered a copy of the first two years of the four-year college curriculum. However, by 1945 they had assumed a two-pronged purpose: that of providing the first two years of college and that of providing advanced technical/vocational training. Many of these were funded by the states that sought to provide the returning GIs, many of whom were married and starting families, with access to higher education within their own communities rather than at a distant state college (Brickman and Lehrer, 1962).

In the 1980s with the elimination of the draft and the beginning of a long period in which the United States was not involved in a major war, the number of people able to take advantage of the GI Bill decreased considerably. However, the concept of providing funding to students had gained acceptance. Thus, at the same time the Civil Rights movement propelled many universities to initiate a policy of open admission, the federal government passed a series of bills providing for student loans and scholarships based on need. Many colleges switched from scholarships based mainly on merit to those based mainly on financial status. In addition, colleges increased the number of students they hired to work while attending classes. The number of working-class students, especially minorities and women, skyrocketed.

However, there were still many children of the working class who could not attend any of these institutions. Shift workers, those who lived in isolated rural areas, and those who were without transportation to and from a college were prevented from attending. Today these barriers are coming down as distance education via the Internet makes a college education accessible to anyone with a computer. Students can "tune in" at any time of the day or night from their homes or places of work to get the lectures, assignments, and handouts, and they have two-way communication with their professors. A number of colleges are offering degrees for programs taken wholly over the Internet. Although this mode of higher education is just beginning, many people, including working-class students, are already taking advantage of it. And the number is expected to continue to increase for some time in the future.

One of the major reasons for this increase is that the need to obtain a college degree over the past quarter of a century has become increasingly important in terms of earning potential and quality of life. The literacy skills needed in a job have changed drastically in many occupations, and increasingly employers require college degrees (Boiarsky, 1997).

Today, workers going into an hourly manufacturing position need to know some basic calculus and physics. They need to be able to write reports, agendas, and minutes for meetings as part of a team, and proposals for change as part of the Total Quality Management (TQM) process introduced into manufacturing, the hotel and restaurant business, banking, and almost every other field. And they have to be able to read these same documents. Moreover, they have to continually learn new skills and strategies as they are likely to follow several different careers in their lifetimes (SCANS Report, 1991). Because of this new environment, Finn (1999) perceives a change in the attitudes of working-class parents toward school as they begin to recognize "education as the only chance for their children's survival" (xii).

Thus, the conditions necessary for college to become available to the working class—a relevant curriculum, funding, and access—have been met. Institutions of higher education today offer curricula that provide working-class students with the skills they need to maintain their jobs and to enrich their lives. Funding to attend these institutions can be obtained through numerous governmental loans; and community colleges, open admissions, and the Internet have made college courses accessible to everyone regardless of their ethnic, cultural, racial, or class background or geographic location. With an increasing number of working-class students able to enroll in colleges and universities and the increasing pressure for these students to acquire a postsecondary education, we need to find ways to prepare them to succeed in the academy. While, in the nineteenth century only those working-class students who showed "special talents" attended college, today many working-class students are matriculating who lack the procedural and contextual knowledge they need. In the next two sections we specifically examine these working-class students and discuss some of the causes of their problems.

Defining Working Class

What do we mean by working class? What are the criteria that define working-class families? Economic? Sociological? Psychological? Educational? Job? Lifestyle? Power? The term has evolved over the years as we have moved from an industrial to a technological society.

Political Definitions

The term "working class" is based in nineteenth-century industrial society when it connoted those engaged in physical labor in contrast to those engaged in mental or supervisory work. Marx extended the definition to encompass a political perspective by establishing a dichotomy between working class (the proletariat) and capitalists (the owners). This concept was further extended by those who saw the dichotomy as that between those without power (workers) and those in control (managers, owners). "Working-class positions are largely differentiated by their lack of autonomy. Clerical workers, factory employees, and other "workers" are all closely supervised; management and professionals do the supervising or work within a peer system" (Fay and Tokarczyk, 1993, p. 5).

But this definition presents several problems in that it fails to recognize that many of those in authoritative positions, such as managers, self-employed consultants, and company executives, are themselves controlled by others, such as a company's CFO, a consultant's clients, and the stockholders, respectively. Linkon (1999) argues that those in positions of management, teaching and, recently, even in medicine also lack autonomy in decision making.

Sociological Definition

Weber, looking to other criteria, suggests that the idea of class encompasses a socioeconomic aspect. "Class represents a group with similar economic life chances...[and a similar] cultural base" (Jackman and Jackman, 1983, p. 2). Research by sociologists during the 1980s reinforced this socioeconomic view. Based on the results of their studies, sociologists perceived classes as composed of groups of people with "similar socio-economic standing," based on their earned income, education, and occupational status, the latter being determined by "prestige, skill [required], job authority and task discretion" (217). Because their studies indicated that members of the working class earned less than the "average" salary as determined by the U.S. Census Bureau, they ranked this group as the second rung in a continuum of five "status groups"— poor, working class, middle class, upper middle class, upper class. However, over the last half of the twentieth century with the help of the unions, many of those whose occupational status placed them in the working-class category have been able to earn as much as those in such professions as teaching and nursing. Thus, income as a criterion for distinguishing between the working class and the middle class is invalidated, and the distinction between the working class and the middle class on the continuum becomes fuzzy.

With economic criteria no longer a valid measure of class, sociologists have turned to cultural factors, such as people's "lifestyle, and beliefs and feelings" (Jackman and Jackman, 1983, 217). These criteria appear more applicable as jobs have expanded to include those in the information/service sector of the economy, noted for their low salaries, and those in the technological sector, noted for their high salaries. Today, we perceive the working class holding blue- and pink-collar jobs that encompass not only working on a line and doing main- tenance but also serving in a restaurant and providing clerical assistance. Lifestyle increasingly appears to play a role in delineating among classes.

Charlip (1995) reminisces about a sociology professor who provides the following criteria to distinguish between working class and middle class. "If you earn thirty thousand dollars a year working in an assembly plant, come home from work, open a beer and watch the game, you are working class; if you earn twenty thousand dollars a year as a school teacher, come home from work to a glass of white wine and PBS, you are middle class" (26).

Both Judith and Julie's families reinforce this concept. As the daughter of a minister/school teacher and a secretary/school library aide, Judith always considered herself as part of the middle class rather than the working class. Her father, heir to a Philadelphia ice cream company, took a step down financially when he decided to go into a seminary instead of into a boardroom. When Judith and her three other siblings were growing up in the 1960s, her father was earning only a few thousand dollars a year plus the use of a parsonage. "My family often seemed to have fewer new things and more hand-me-downs than the working class children in the neighborhood. We were living a life of 'gen- teel poverty,' " she comments wryly. "We were always pinching pennies, bor- rowing books from the library rather than buying them from a bookstore. But the life of the mind was a priority and all four of us expected to go to college and have professional careers."

Julie's family also seems to defy a neat definition of working class, al- though economically her family can be considered part of that class. Her father still works their farm, and her mother maintains her nursing license, though she "nurses" only at voluntary functions like blood banks. But they have a middle- class view of education. Julie grew up watching her parents read magazines and newspapers to learn about agriculture, farm management, health and nutri- tion, and computers.

In an attempt to classify people like Judith and Julie's parents who either fall in the gap between the various classes or who overlap them, Rogers and Teixeira (2000) suggest using the four-year college degree as the basis for dif- ferentiating between the two classes and using the type of work created by the difference in education to distinguish between the two groups. Thus, they would replace the term "middle class," which implies an economic level, with the term "professional class," which implies an educational level. Using this classification system, they draw the following profile of today's working class.

- About two-fifths have some education beyond high school; about one-tenth hold an associate degree.
- They are mainly low-level white-collar and service workers or skilled blue-collar workers.

- The median household income is $42,000—the low side of what is considered a middle-class income.
- They live in and dominate the suburbs.
- They are mainly two-earner income families.

Thus, it would appear that people can hold professional positions, even though the pay they receive places them in a low economic level or they can hold jobs that fall into the working-class category because the positions do not require a four-year education, but the pay may place them economically in the middle class. Linkon (1999) suggests it is the difference between having a "job" and having a "career."

Psychological Definition

Peter Stillman, former editor of Boynton/Cook Publishers, believes that class may be as much a psychological phenomenon as it is an economic and educational one. He cites the difference between his background and mine as an example. Both of my parents—the children of working-class families—went to college. My father, an optometrist, had been the son of an optician, and my mother, a teacher, had been the daughter of a postal clerk. I didn't consider them any different from the students of working-class families today. Yet, Peter perceives a world of difference between them and his own parents. His father had been a carpenter and his mother a housewife. The difference, he argues, resides in the families' perceptions of education. "Your grandparents raised your father and mother to go on to higher education and leave the working class." His grandparents had not raised their children to attend college. For him, the difference was not only whether or not a person had had a college education but whether a college education was perceived as a route to leaving the working class. College often appears so far removed from many working-class parents, because of either cost or lifestyle, that they never even consider it. It is from families such as these that many of the recently published stories of working-class academics emanate (Brodkey, 1984; Shor, 1980).

One of these stories comes from Irvin Peckham (1995), whose father was an auto mechanic. He explains, "Students from the professional/managerial class are learning to think, speak, and write in ways that are reinforced by their homes and communities, while working-class students have to make significant breaks with their families' and communities' patterns of language and thought" (264). Peckham suggests using educational attainment and job classification as the key criteria for determining class, as these factors have the greatest effect on children's ability to adapt to the academy (264). Ashley (2001) adopts Peckham's criteria for her study of successful working-class students, defining these students as those who "come from families where parents work at physical labor jobs and who are also the first in their immediate families to attend or complete a college degree" (499).

Relationship with Ethnicity/Race and Immigration

A discussion of "working class" cannot be concluded until we consider the relationship between ethnicity/race and class. Julie has found that many people believe the working class is composed mainly of racial minorities and immigrants. However, the majority of the working-class population is from white native-born families (Rogers and Teixeira, 2000). Most of the students at Purdue University Calumet fall into this category. Linkon (1999) believes the perception to which Julie refers may be the result of geographic location. She suggests that in urban centers, such as Chicago and New York, where a large number of immigrants and people of color live, this perception of the working class may be valid, but in rural areas, such as Minnesota, Indiana, and Arkansas, the majority of the working class is "almost exclusively white, Northern European and Protestant" (5).

Julie argues that people tend to relate ethnicity/race and class, because class seems to make ethnicity or race more "visible." She points out that class can often be a determinant of acceptable behavior. For example, middle-class students are perceived as being cosmopolitan if they study a second language in school, but working-class students who grow up in homes where languages other than English are spoken often believe they have to downplay their bilingualism. She notes that ESL students try very hard to "lose" an accent and to adopt "correct" American speech patterns, whereas middle-class students are very comfortable with their dialects (Valdés, 1992). Linkon (1999) agrees. She suggests that class image may be based on such visible characteristics as clothing or housing, as much as on jobs, education, and earning power. Julie also perceives class image being based on linguistic markers. Peckham (1995) notes that working-class students are marked by such "substandard" language as "ain't," "he don't," and the use of "me" in the position of a predicate subject.

Even if we qualify ethnicity as a characteristic of the working class by stating "those in the working class are *often* members of an ethnic group," we are failing to recognize that we're all members of ethnic groups. Immigrants from around the world—Ireland, Poland, Germany, Africa, etc.—have been coming to this country and attending our schools since its inception. More recently people have emigrated from Eastern Europe, the Mideast, India, Pakistan, Vietnam, Cambodia, Korea, Ethiopia, and Kenya. Although these new immigrants come from all segments of society, they often start out in this country in working-class jobs. Because of the language barrier or because of requirements for certification in certain American professions, such as medicine or accounting, these immigrant families are often forced to take low-paying jobs when they first arrive here, though they may have been engineers or doctors in their native countries. However, while they may evidence some of the socioeconomic features of the working class, they don't exhibit the features related to lifestyle; rather they more closely fit Rogers and Teixeira's definition of the "professional class" (2000).

Those immigrants who were professionals in their homeland but were forced to take working-class jobs over here because of their lack of proficiency in English or inability to secure professional certification in this country still have the accumulated literacy of the middle class to pass on to their children. These children, who are likely to be literate in their first language, to be schooled in their home country, and perhaps even to have studied English in school in their home country, are likely to do fine in American schools. They just need a few years to become fluent in English. On the other hand, children of immigrant parents of lesser means are less likely to be literate in their first language, less likely to have stable school histories, and less likely to have studied English before they arrive. Without a strong background, these children are more likely to struggle in school (Greenberg, Macias, and Rhodes, 2001).

A Two-Tiered Working Class

From these discussions the difficulty in defining the "working class" becomes apparent, especially as many members of the working class perceive themselves as members of the middle class (Vanneman, 1983). In an effort to take into account the various inconsistencies presented in this section, we would like to suggest that the working class is composed of two tiers—those who fall into the traditional category of physical laborers, who earn little money and have minimal decision-making authority; and Rogers and Teixeira's "working middle class," composed of nonprofessionals who do not have a four-year college education. It is the children of these two subclasses, those who are the first generation to attend college, to whom we refer in our discussions of working-class students.

Characteristics of Working-Class Students

For the most part working-class students who struggle in school, those whom Dickson (1995) calls "novice learners," come to us with a different set of literacy practices from those of the professional class.[2] By recognizing the following sociological, cultural, and psychological sites from which these students arrive at college, we can better understand their difficulties in adapting to an academic environment.

- They have grown up in families who earn less than the median income earned by professional families.
- Their parents work in blue-/pink-collar or nonprofessional service jobs.
- They are first-generation college students.

- They exist in an authoritarian environment, with little control over decisions related to their lives. (Decisions related to work are made by management and decisions related to their lifestyles are made by parents.)
- They live in a world governed by rules and procedures.
- They work at jobs rather than in careers, perceiving the job not as an end in and of itself but rather as a means to pay for their life outside of work.
- They are often paid by the hour with time becoming a measure of their worth.

The attitudes of working-class students toward the academy and their responses to academic requirements are closely related to these sites.

Influence of Family

Many working-class parents perceive education solely as a means for their children to move up the economic ladder; they seldom recognize that a college's goals are far broader than job training and that, therefore, their children need far more knowledge than just that required for a job. One of the reasons for this perception is that they think of work in terms of a job rather than as a career. A job is something that is done in order to make enough money to pay for the things they would prefer doing.

During discussions with her developmental reading and introductory literature classes, Judith found over and over again that students perceive the primary reason for getting a degree is to get a good job and earn more money. But she also found they wanted more. That they were thinking in terms of a career rather than a job. They indicated they wanted opportunities, both professionally and personally, that their parents never had. As one student expressed it, "I came to college so that when I have a family of my own, I won't have to struggle like my parents did. I want to go to a job that I like every day. So I study the field that interests me most. I want to be better than my parents. My father never graduated and doesn't know how to read. He can never work anywhere but where he is now."

Because many working-class parents do not understand the academic culture, their children do not have the kind of help children of professional families have in making the transition to the academy. Although these parents, especially those who have immigrated here, may be supportive of their children's decision to go on to higher education, in many cases they are unfamiliar with an academic environment, and their perceptions of college may differ strikingly from reality. Clement Stacy, a professor of American literature at Purdue University Calumet, tells the story of a young Greek girl who was his student. One day he received a telephone call from her father who insisted on meeting with him. The father arrived in tie and jacket and treated him with great deference. Once the introductions were out of the way, the father rather uncomfortably approached the subject that had brought him to the meeting. It seemed that his daughter felt that she did not need to go to school every day. In fact, she had told him that she did not remain in class all day during the days she went. Was this true? He wanted to find out about this. His daughter had always told him the truth, but he had difficulty understanding this.

As Stillman points out in the previous section, so much depends on the home environment. As I think back to my own upbringing, I realize that from the time I entered elementary school, I was being prepared to enter the academic dialog. I remember sitting around the dinner table listening to my parents and grandparents, who lived with us, discuss the events of the day—the Eisenhower versus Stevenson campaign, the Kefauver hearings, etc. This was not a passive experience. My sister and I were encouraged to ask questions and participate. To do so, we were expected to listen to newscasts on the radio and later television and to read the newspaper.

Many working-class students, however, seldom have any such opportunities. As first-generation college students, they often have no one who can model what they need to do, how they need to participate, or " how to play the game." I became aware of this lack of role models several years ago when I attended the twenty-fifth reunion of my junior high school class, which had been composed of a rather remarkable group of students, representing both working- and professional-class backgrounds. Many of the members had gone on to become eminent in their fields, including the famous natural healer Dr. Andrew Weil; Dr. Michael Shelansky, Chair and Delafield Professor of Pathology at Columbia University; Stephanie Weiss Naidoff, LLB Vice President and General Council for Thomas Jefferson University; Juliet Goodfriend, winner of the Greater Philadelphia Chamber of Commerce Paradigm Award for outstanding professional and personal achievement as founder and CEO of Strategic Marketing Corp., and the Honorable Carol Agin Kipperman, Judge in Cook County (Chicago), Illinois. At the reunion, the group of about twenty sat in a circle, telling stories about what the class had meant to them. Susan Pomerantz, the owner of a number of nursing homes in the Philadelphia area, commented that through the class she had been introduced to a whole new kind of literacy. For the first time she had been in homes where there were hard-backed books. The only reading materials she'd ever seen in her home were the condensed novels published by Readers' Digest and paperback mysteries.

Finn (1999) talks about the kinds of reading materials children of working-class parents, like Susan, see in their homes. He comments, "The children of the working class learn to read and write in classrooms whose discourse mirrors their homes and communities, but they do not make progress toward informational and powerful literacy. Their progress ends with functional or perhaps informational literacy" (126).

Authoritarian Environment

The influence of family appears to be one of the major causes of students' reticence in taking an active part in their education. In most Hispanic, Mediterranean, Eastern European, Middle Eastern, and Asian cultures the family is run by the parents, usually the father, who establishes the rules and, unlike the more permissive American Spock-influenced culture, these parents expect to be obeyed without lengthy explanations.[3] Peckham (1995) notes that "the authoritarian environment of the working class discourages them [the working class] from questioning" and "because of the infrequent dialectal discourse in the home, working class students do not learn how to qualify and substantiate assertions" (99).

When Judith surveyed her students about the skills they needed to succeed at college, most placed the ability to think more critically and more independently at the top of their lists. One student wrote, "Once they [students] get to the university level there is no one to hold their hand. . . . That is how college and real life is. Not someone standing over you telling you what and how to do things." While her students identify thinking critically as an expectation for succeeding in college, they don't know how to learn to do it. They admit to her that it is difficult for them to 'think different.'"

This acceptance of authority and adherence to rules is further enforced in the workplace where rules and procedures are established by management, which passes them down to supervisors who enforce them on the plant floor. Shor (1997) notes that this authoritative structured work environment and family orientation may also be the cause of students' difficulty in adjusting to a flexible-style classroom. Students often have difficulty getting assignments in on time without constant reminding or reading assigned texts that are not reviewed by an instructor. Students used to a structured workplace find themselves afloat in chaos in a flexible classroom environment. Shor talks about his problems in initiating a flexible-style, process-oriented, student-centered classroom when he first began teaching. He readily admits that his students did worse than when he had used a structured approach. What he found he needed to do was to wean them from the security of a teacher-centered, rule-based, procedure-driven environment into one in which they assumed the responsibility for their own learning. Rather than throw them on their own resources from the first day of classes, he constructed Bruner's scaffold and slowly began to give them more and more freedom until, by the final assignment, he let them make decisions on their own.

Students from a structured environment not only have difficulty adapting to a flexible one but also find the lack of authority in a student-centered classroom disconcerting. Many have difficulty understanding the sources of authority in this kind of environment and often respond with a lack of respect for the instructor. Finn (1999, p. 3) comments, "They expect people in authority to be authoritarian." I have had students leave my technical writing class shaking their heads because I have not/will not tell them the "correct" way to write a proposal or to set up a comparison/contrast section. "You'll have to try it both ways (aabb or abab) I tell them in relation to the latter and see which one 'works.'" How can I be an authority, their head shaking implies, if I can't tell them which it is.

Relationship Between Work and School

This emphasis on functional literacy can have a powerful influence on working-class students' perceptions of the academy. According to Judith, a commonly held view of the academy is that it is a place distinct from the "real world," a kind of intellectual playground where people "play around" for a few years before getting down to the "real" business of life.

Judith surmises that this may be why students often think reading fiction or narrative is a leisure activity rather than an academic or informational one. Part of their resistance to academic discourse may be the perception that much of what is done in the academy seems like "goofing off." She recalls telling the students in a developmental reading course about a book she read in which the author narrates his story of driving around the country with Einstein's brain (Paterniti, 2000). Although her students were interested and even amused by the story, they admitted that they wouldn't have spent the time to read it. She had the time to read this sort of story, but they didn't.

This phenomenon can be observed in the way in which working-class students perceive time. Students bring to the academy a perception of time that is analogous to their workplace. Because many working-class people are paid hourly wages, working-class students often perceive their courses in terms of the hours they spend in class rather than as information learned. Absences and tardiness are regarded as infractions against the company in terms of rules related to time rather than as losses in terms of information not received. A college degree is perceived as much a measure of hours put in as information learned.

Defining Academic Literacy

Much has already been written about academic literacy (Ashley, 2001; Brodkey, 1989; Finn, 1999; Linkon, 1999; Rose, 1989; Shor, 1996; Weese, Fox, and Greene, 1999). This section attempts to synthesize these previous discussions and to present an overview of the main aspects of academic literacy on which most of those who have examined the subject appear to agree.

"Academic literacy" is as difficult to define as "working class." This is in part because literacy is more than simply the rules of phonology, morphology, semantics, and syntax. It's more than simply decoding or encoding the language on the page. Rather, language/literacy entails "ways of being in the world." It represents an agreed-on set of conventions for "behaving, interacting, valuing, thinking, believing, speaking, and often reading and writing." It "incorporates a usually taken for granted and tacit 'theory' of what is the 'right' way to think, feel, and behave." To be literate, students must not only say the "right thing" but they must express the "right" beliefs, values, and attitudes (Gee, 1996, pp. viii–ix, 124).

Thus, literacy involves procedural and contextual knowledge as well as content knowledge. Finn (1999) believes that the purpose of literacy is to teach students "procedures and invite them to create their own procedures or make our procedures more congenial to themselves or more useful to themselves" as well as to teach them "the attitudes and behaviors of powerful people regarding authority, conformity, isolation, and power, which in turn make the use of explicit language sensible and necessary" (126–7).[4]

If definitions of literacy include beliefs, attitudes, and habits of mind, then a definition of academic literacy must necessarily include a belief in critical thinking; the value placed on reading and writing to do the work of the university, the emphasis placed on independence, self-reliance, and responsibility; and the close relationship between the work done and the ideas debated in school and a person's ability to perform a job later on. But academic literacy goes beyond this. It also involves knowledge-making. As members of the academy, students must process, comprehend, and respond to existing knowledge—in short, make it their own—and make new knowledge. Using the metaphor of conversation, students must listen to the talk going on around them, figure out how and when it's best to jump into the conversation, and then add to the discussion when it's their turn.

Students who are academically literate know that "the academic community is a *community*, that its members converse with one another on paper, and that their job is to become a member of that community. To be a member requires that they "go beyond discovering and expressing their own ideas. They must recognize the concerns of the community as a whole, to analyze the terms of the various conversations going on within it, and to identify the ground rules for participating in each conversation." Furthermore they must recognize that "the conversation in some cases has been going on for centuries (e.g., discussions about the nature of justice), and that in order to participate, they must understand what has already been said, in addition to what is currently being said." To become academically literate, students must "learn to recognize how a conversation focuses on a particular issue; learn to explore that issue, against a background of assumed familiarity with related issues; learn how to analyze someone else's remarks to see in what part of what conversation they belong; and learn to fit their own ideas and experiences into the conversation" (Jones, 1992, pp. 55–6).

Academic literacy and creativity, according to Julie, are often defined in very similar terms. Creativity is defined as looking at something familiar in a new way or making a connection between two known pieces of information that have never been connected before. It's a tension between the old and the new, the familiar and the never-before-seen (Csikszentmihalyi, 1996; Goleman, Kaufman, & Ray, 1992). Creativity isn't about coming up with a completely new idea, as most people think. Rather, it's about locating oneself in a domain of knowledge and then pushing the boundaries of that domain— by expanding the boundaries, turning them inside out, intersecting them with the boundaries of other domains, etc. This definition of creativity makes sense—students can't "think outside the box," to use a buzz word for creativity from business, if there's no "box" to begin with, or if they don't go "outside" it.

The same can be said of academic literacy. Academics preserve the knowledge of the past by understanding it (and passing it on to students, who in turn make it their own) and make new knowledge in part by critically interrogating past knowledge. Students must do the same. In college, students are expected to *re-present*—recast and use for their own purposes—knowledge they've accepted as true because there were good reasons for believing it. Thus, in college, they're asked to both submit and resist: not just summarize a text, but also respond to it; not just describe or explain it, but analyze, interpret, or evaluate it; not just restate a source text, but displace it with their own (Bartholcmae, 1985). Finn (1999) insists that literacy must include the highest levels of knowledge-making—synthesis and evaluation (Bloom, 1956).

For students to engage in this way, they must accept certain beliefs about the nature of knowledge: that knowledge is created; that they themselves are capable of creating knowledge; that authors present knowledge in the form of claims rather than truths; that the knowledge claims of one author often conflict with those of another; and that they can test knowledge claims and decide which are worthy of acceptance because they're backed by good reasons (Penrose & Geisler, 1994).

Julie suggests that it is not that working-class students come to college "unprepared," it is just that they are prepared for a different environment. She believes that if we think of our students as "unprepared," then we see them as lacking. We ignore what they know and can do and focus only on what they can't do. If we recognize that they have literacy skills—even though those skills may be different from the ones we value in the academy—then we can see students as already competent in important ways and as having the potential to learn new ways if they want. There is a cultural difference in perceptions here as opposed to a lack of effort. When we recognize the literacy skills students already have, then we're more likely to find ways to tap into that literacy to help them develop academic literacy practices. Julie tells her basic writing students that she knows they already know how to read and write, but she's there to help them learn to read and write *on the college level,* to meet the expectations of their academic audience. She uses what she calls a pedagogy of overt comparison to help students sort out the similarities and differences between the literacy practices they already use and the ones they need to acquire.

Julie believes that all students can acquire academic literacy though they may struggle with it at first. For this reason she advocates a rigorous curriculum for her basic writing course. She starts with literacies working-class students bring from home. But she doesn't stop there. She moves on to tasks that ask students to practice analysis, synthesis, evaluation, concession, refutation, etc. Thus, she tries to provide writing assignments that generally involve a response to a situation or a text.[5] She wants her students to understand the text, the problem posed, and the solution offered, and to write a composition that displaces the response of the sources with one of their own that takes these others into account. She asks rhetorically "If we don't motivate and challenge students to set projects they might not set for themselves, then we ask them merely to rehearse what they already know. Where's the learning in that?" (See Chapter 8 for Julie's strategies.)

Novice Academics

As the discussions in this chapter indicate, not only has the perception changed of who the working class are, but also there is no longer a simple set of criteria to define them. It is impossible to perceive this class as a single, monolithic group when minority and immigrant status, ethnic background and geographic location appear to create differences in the behaviors and attitudes of this so-called class. Furthermore, when looking at power and economics, the traits of today's working class spill over into the middle or professional classes. Therefore, rather than adopt the "I know it when I see it" concept, this book's focus extends beyond the borders of a specific class to be concerned with all of those people who exhibit at least some of the characteristics that have been discussed in this chapter. Furthermore, it is evident that the students of the working class are not alone in their lack of academic literacy but that many children of the professional or middle classes also arrive at college without an understanding of the values of the academic community or the knowledge and skills, attitudes and traits they need to succeed in that community. Thus, the concepts discussed in this book and the methods and activities suggested can be applied to all students who are "novice academics," regardless of their economic or social class, regardless of whether they are native-born Americans or immigrants, regardless of whether they are mono- or multicultural/multilingual, and regardless of the literacies they bring with them to schools.

Our job, as teachers, is to prepare these students to succeed in college English, to help them place the "squat pen" between their finger and thumb and "dig with it."

Notes

1. The University of Georgia was actually the first state university, but it didn't receive sufficient funding until a number of years later.

2. Not all students of the professional class arrive at college with academic literacy. Belanger and Panozzo point this out in Chapter 5 in this book.

3. An interesting deviation can be seen in the ability of some working-class Jewish women who are quite comfortable entering into lively intellectual debates. Tannen (1993) found that middle eastern Jewish families encouraged their children, both sons and daughters, to participate in intellectual discussions held at the dinner table.

4. Finn (1999) along with Boiarsky (1997) argues that a higher level of literacy is necessary for people whether they are going on to college or into the workplace, but this discussion is not part of this book.

5. The paradigmatic text in the academy generally begins with a problem, includes a review of the solutions offered/tried, a discussion of why these solutions are inadequate, and finally an argument for a new response.

References

Ashley, Hannah. 2001. "Playing the Game: Proficient Working-Class Student Writers' Second Voices." *Research in the Teaching of English*. 35: 493–522.

Bartholomae, David. 1985. "Against the Grain." In *Writers on Writing*, edited by Tom Waldrep, 18–29. New York: Random House.

Bennett, Michael. 2000. *When Dreams Came True*. Washington, DC: Brassey's.

Bloom, Benjamin, S. 1956. *Taxonomy of Educational Objectives*. New York: David McKay Company, Inc.

Boiarsky, Carolyn. 1997. *The Art of Workplace English*. Portsmouth, NH: Boynton/Cook Publishers.

Brodkey, Linda. 1994. "Writing on the Bias." *College English*. 56: 527–47.

Callahan, Raymond E. 1957. *An Introduction to Education in American Society*. New York: Alfred A. Knopf.

Csikszentmihalyi, Mihalyi. 1996. *Creativity: Flow and the Psychology of Discovery and Invention.* New York: Harper Collins.

DeCicco, Charles. 1997. The City College of New York Sesquicentennial. New York: CCNY Publications.

Dews, C. L. Barney, and Carolyn Leste Law (Eds.) 1995. *This Fine Place So Far From Home.* Philadelphia: Temple University Press.

Dickson, Marcia. 1995. *It's Not Like That Here*. Portsmouth, NH: Boynton/Cook Publishers.

Finn, Patrick J. 1999. *Literacy with an Attitude: Educating Working-Class Children in Their Own Self-Interest.* Albany, NY: State University of New York Press, 1999.

Garraty, John A. 1981. *A Short History of the American Nation*. New York: Harper and Row Publishers.

Gee, James Paul. 1996. *Social Linguistics and Literacies: Ideology in Discourses*. 2nd ed. Bristol, PA: Taylor & Francis.

Goleman, Daniel, Paul, Kaufman, and Michael L. Ray. 1992. *The Creative Spirit*. New York: Dutton.

Greenberg, Elizabeth, Reynaldo F. Macias, David Rhodes, and Tsze Chan. 2001. *English Literacy and Language Minorities in the United States*. Washington, DC: U.S. Department of Education.

Grossman, Ron, and Charles Leroux.1998. "Reading, Writing and Reeboks." *Chicago Tribune*, Tempo, Section 5 (May 7, 1998) 1–7.

Hofstadter, Richard, and Wilson Smith. 1961. *American Higher Education: A Documentary History.* Chicago: University of Chicago Press.

Horowitz, Helen, L. 1987. *Campus life: Undergraduate Cultures from the End of the Eighteenth Century to the Present.*Chicago: University of Chicago Press.

Jones, Gary L. 1992. "Playing across the Curriculum: Freshman Writing as an Introduction to Writing in the Disciplines." *Issues in Writing* 5: 54–76.

Linkon, Sherry Lee. 1999. "Introduction." In *Teaching Working Class,* edited by Sherry Lee Linkon, Amherst, MA: University of Massachusetts Press. i–xi.

Paterniti, Michael. 2000. *Driving Mr. Albert: A Trip Across America with Einstein's Brain.* New York: Random House.

Peckham, Irwin. 1995. "Complicity in Class Codes: The Exclusionary Function of Education." In *This Fine Place So Far From Home,* edited by C.L. B. Dews and C. L. Law. Philadelphia: Temple University Press. 263-275.

Penn Web Steering Committee. 2001. Penn about Penn: A Historical Perspective. www.upenn.edu.

Penrose, Ann M., and Cheryl Geisler. 1994. "Reading and Writing Without Authority." *College Composition and Communication* 45: 505–20.

Pfinster, Allan O. 1962. "A Century of the Church-Related College." In *A Century of Higher Education,* edited by William W. Brickman and Stanley Lehrer, 80–93. New York: Society for the Advercement of Education.

Rogers, Joel, and Ruy Teixeira. 2000. "America's Forgotten Majority." *Atlantic Monthly* 285.6: 66–75.

Rose, Mike. 1989. *Lives on the Boundary.* New York: Penguin Books.

Schmidt, George. 1962. "A Century of the Liberal Arts College." In *A Century of Higher Education,* edited by William W. Brickman and Stanley Lehrer, 50–66.

Secretary's Commission on Achieving Necessary Skills [SCANS]. 1991. What Work Requires of Schools: A SCANS Report for America 2000. Washington, DC: U.S. Department of Labor.

Shor, Ira. 1996. *When Students Have Power: Negotiating Authority in a Critical Pedagogy.* Chicago: University of Chicago Press.

———. 1997. Discussion at Conference on Working Class Studies. Youngstown, Ohio.

Stacy, Clement, and Michael Dobberstein. 1999. Responses by Colleges and Universities to the GI Bill. Presented Popular Culture Conference, Manhattan, KS.

Tannen, Deborah. 1993. *Gender and Conversational Interaction.* New York: Oxford University Press.

Tokarczyk, Michelle M., and Elizabeth A. Fay. (Eds.). 1993. *Working Class Women in the Academy: Laborers in the Knowledge Factory.* Amherst, MA: University of Massachusetts Press.

Valdés, Guadalupe. 1992. "Bilingual Minorities and Language Issues in Writing: Toward Profession Wide Responses to a New Challenge." *Written Communication* 9: 85–136.

Weese, Katherine, Stephen Fox, and Stuart Greene. 1999. *Teaching Academic Literacy.* Mahwah, NJ: Erlbaum.

2

Learning to Learn

Helping Students Become Independent Thinkers

Carolyn Boiarsky

The illiterates of the future are not those who cannot read or write.
They are those who cannot learn, unlearn, and relearn.

—Alvin Toffler

Tim is typical of many working-class students. Having found that he had little aptitude for studying during his twelve years of public schooling, he took
a job in the family's construction business once he graduated high school. But,
after several years, he realized he was going nowhere—his college-educated
siblings were making more money and taking on more responsibility in the
business—so he decided to enroll at a nearby college. Despite his having to
spend the first few years taking remedial courses, the decision proved to be a
good one.

Tim's generation is the first in his family to attend college. Like most
students of working-class families, Tim has continued to work while taking
one or two courses each semester. Slowly, he has plodded through the basic
core curriculum, eventually declaring a major. It will probably be several
more years before he completes a degree. But there is no doubt that he will
graduate.

I've watched Tim grow over the past seven years. Not physically. He is still
the slight, gangling boy (not such a boy at twenty-nine) that he was when he first
enrolled in the University. But he has grown academically. He took developmental English, the course provided for students whose entrance tests are too low for
placement in the regular freshman composition course, three times. But he never
gave up: "I keep getting closer," he told his advisor after each semester. Eventually he passed. In fact, he "got hold" of the whole idea of writing well enough to

become a professional writing major. His problem in the course on "Desktop Publishing" wasn't with writing, but with getting control over the computer. On his second try at that course, he passed. This term in my class in "Writing Computer Documentation," he got an A. The first time. Somewhere, in the middle of the term, he made the connection between what he had learned in the beginning of the course and what he needed to know for the remainder of the course.

It was not an easy course. Students were learning to write documentation for software programs, such as the latest upgrade for MS Word or Lotus' CC:Mail. Students were assigned a task, such as creating a page with two columns, and then required to write the instructions for doing it. Each set of instructions comprised a module of a documentation manual. In the beginning of the course, students worked on modules for tasks that they knew how to do, such as deleting a sentence. As the course progressed, they began to write modules for tasks with which they were not familiar, such as inserting a graph from Excel into a Word file.

"We have to include the same kinds of information in this project that we included in the first one?" Tim half stated, half asked as he worked on the advanced module. "Like tips and warnings? But this time it has to relate to this project?"

He stood in my office doorway, looking for approval, ready to recognize he had been mistaken as he had been so often in his academic career. But this time he was right. He had recognized that the criteria (the audience's knowledge of the topic and purpose for reading the document) that I gave the class in the beginning of the semester for determining the content, focus, and style of a module for a software manual related not just to the manual for the first project but to every manual I assigned.

More than any of my other students, Tim would appear outside my office to check on a decision he had made related to a document. Each time I would ask why he had made the decision, and each time he would explain how he had thought through various alternatives, considering the consequences of each. Each time his choice had been a good one, based on the appropriate heuristic—determining the users' needs.

Tim perceived the module he was documenting as a problem to be solved—how to find the best way for the user to accomplish the task—rather than as a writing assignment that could be completed by applying a set of rules. This perception led him to recognize that the problems in the first project were analogous to those in the second and therefore that he could transfer the strategies that he had learned for accomplishing the first project to accomplishing the next one. When he discovered that to accomplish one step the user could enter information in more than one way, he was faced with deciding whether or not to provide the user with a choice. In an effort to solve this problem, he thought back to how he had dealt with a similar problem in the first project. Having learned from the results of the usability test for that project that users become confused when given choices, he concluded that he should provide only a single route when he wrote his second project.

Tim was also aware that problem solving required considering a number of possible solutions rather than being satisfied with the first one he considered. He knew, too, that he needed to examine each alternative, that he must question his choice in terms of its effects in order to arrive at the most effective solution. Thus, he had considered three possibilities: (1) offering the alternatives on an equal basis by providing the users with a decision box from which they could decide which route to take, (2) eliminating the second alternative altogether, or (3) providing the second alternative as a marginal note. He finally decided to include the alternative instruction as a marginal note after realizing that some users would prefer the alternative.

By perceiving writing as a problem-solving activity, recognizing that he could transfer strategies from one problem to a similar one, and assuming a persistent and questioning attitude toward his solutions, Tim had learned to learn.

The remainder of this chapter examines how students learn to learn and the strategies that we need to help students acquire so they will learn to learn. We will look specifically at the strategies for learning to read and write texts and then examine how students can learn to transfer knowledge from one assignment to another, from one course to the next. We will discuss their need to acquire higher order cognitive skills and to assume an appropriate attitude toward learning. Finally we will consider how we can develop lesson plans to integrate learning to learn within our English curriculum.

Learning to Learn

Learning to learn is the very basis for acquiring literacy in any content area. Projections estimate that people will follow five careers in a single lifetime. The ability to acquire new skills for using new technologies and to learn new vocabularies and new content information for new fields is a necessity if today's students are to succeed in tomorrow's world. Learning how to learn may be "the single most important goal of education—in order that students might be prepared to go on learning throughout life" (Brown, paraphrasing Bruner, 1996, p. 79).

What do we mean when we say Tim had learned to learn? What exactly had he learned to do?

Over the years Tim had learned a lot about learning. He had learned to apply problem-solving strategies, such as using his prior experiences and knowledges, like those he had gained in his desktop publishing course, for learning a new course. He had also learned analogical reasoning, which allowed him to successfully transfer the knowledges he had acquired from the desktop publishing course to the new course in software documentation by relating comparable aspects that underlay both of them. Thus, he had recognized that he could transfer the strategies related to format and layout that he had learned in desktop publishing to preparing a page for a documentation module. Not only had he learned how to use the skills he had acquired from previous assignments and courses, but also he had learned to learn from his failures, correcting previous errors and then checking to make certain he did not repeat them in new assignments. Finally, he had learned that he was responsible for his own learning and that it took a lot of persistence on his part to learn. He had recognized the need to spend time thinking about how to fulfill a writing assignment before he ever began writing it and then studying his text with an open mind, doubting and questioning what he had written in order to determine whether the document included all of the necessary conditions and aspects involved in the assignment or whether he needed to consider alternatives to his focus, content, organization, style, voice, or format.

In a general sense, learning to learn means that students can enter a classroom and, regardless of the teacher's teaching style or the subject matter being taught, know how to select and use appropriate strategies to understand the course content sufficiently to discuss, read, and write about it. In learning to learn, students must become active learners, and their goals need to encompass the acquisition of strategies as well as content. Feathers and White (1987) suggest that learning to learn implies that students know the factors that influence comprehension as well as the strategies for comprehending a subject and that students can actively select from among various strategies those that are appropriate for learning a specific subject area. Weinstein (1996) sees learning how to learn as the ability to convert new information into meaningful knowledge that can be used for higher order reasoning tasks and that can be transferred to new demands and contexts, whereas Brown (1996) implies that it is students' knowledge of inquiry skills related to asking strategic questions and then synthesizing and evaluating the responses to arrive at a conclusion.

As a professional writer for the past thirty years, I have become adept at learning how to learn new subject areas. Working as a freelancer, I have written newsletters, brochures, and documentary films in the areas of electrical power, art, sex education, and educational evaluation techniques for professionals in those fields. I have revised documents in nuclear power for nuclear engineers and in computer information systems for MIS employees. I've created brochures for sales staffs in attic ventilation and photographic development equipment, and I've published research articles in professional linguistics journals. Most of the technical writers I know have had English or journalism backgrounds and have never studied the fields in which they are now employed. Nor is this situation limited to professional writers. Marketing research analysts write reports in such disparate fields as pharmacology, cosmetology, and plastic piping. Yet, most of them received a degree in marketing, not in pharmacology, chemistry, or engineering. How do these people acquire the technical vocabulary and field-specific conventions for reading and writing in these fields? The answer is that they learned to learn. They had acquired the strategies for learning to read and write in the new content areas in which they found themselves.

It is this ability to learn to learn as they are confronted with new tasks, new jobs, new careers that is so important to the success of all students. Yet it is one of the least understood aspects of education, especially among working-class and, in fact, most students.

Why is it that so few of our students are able to acquire new knowledge without our serving as intermediaries? The answer is that we have not required them to do so nor have we taught them how to do it. Yet many of us were never taught these strategies. Why then are we finding we must teach them to our students? The reason lies partially with our students' culture and partially with the present school environment.

As we discussed in Chapter 1, many of our students come from homes in which parents are to be respected and obeyed. Implied in this rule is the concept that parents know better than children, that they know what is RIGHT, and in fact, that they know the answers to everything that a child needs to know. Our students bring this concept to school and transfer their parents' role of all-knowing leader to the teacher. They believe that the answers to questions can be found either in their textbooks or through their teachers. Students know that when they fail to answer appropriately, teachers can and do provide the correct response. Teachers usually wait less than a minute after posing a question before providing students with an answer. Students are unfamiliar with situations in which questions are posed that have no absolute answers and in which adults are willing to accept several, often conflicting, points of view. That teachers might ask questions for which they do not know the answers is unimaginable. When students come across this situation for the first time, often not until they are in college, they are taken aback and may even consider the teacher "stupid." They reason that if a teacher is teaching a course, she should know the answers to questions related to the course. However, in college composition and literature courses, the answers to questions are not simply to be found in paragraph 3 on page 10. In fact, if students do no more than restate an idea from a chapter in a textbook, they will usually not receive a grade higher than a C. To get a higher grade, college students are expected to dig deeper. But many students are not even aware that this is what they must do. And even if they are aware, they do not know how. Dig where? And with what? They have no idea. Nor have most of them developed the persistence required to do so.

Yet college teachers, regardless of content area, expect that students arrive at a university knowing the strategies that Tim had acquired. By the time students enroll in a college course, they are expected to recognize that they will need to expend a great deal of effort in learning and that they will be required to demonstrate depth in their thinking and quality in their performance. Bruner's scaffold has been dismantled; students are expected to stand on their own (Bruner, 1979). Thus, the need to provide students with the strategies, heuristics, attitudes, and knowledges that will enable them to take responsibility for their own learning so that they can succeed when they enter institutions of higher education should underlie all instruction from kindergarten through high school.

Reading and Writing as Problem-Solving Tasks

We seldom think of reading and writing as problem-solving tasks. But if students are to understand that they can transfer the knowledge that they acquire from one literature assignment to another, from one writing assignment to another, then they need to perceive their courses as more than the acquisition of pieces of information and sets of rules. They need to recognize that in literature classes they are not just "learning *Macbeth*" or "learning *The Bluest Eye,*" but that they are learning to understand and interpret various kinds of literatures; they are not simply "learning persuasive writing" but learning to write persuasively. They need to perceive their assignments as problems to be solved rather than as templates in which information can simply be inserted according to some set of rules. Newell and Simon (1972) define a problem as "something a person wants but does not know immediately what series of actions to perform to get it." By applying this definition to reading and writing, we can easily perceive these tasks as problems. In reading a poem, we want to know how to interpret the text; in writing an essay, we want to know how to organize our information to create a coherent text. Thus, reading and writing require as much critical thinking as a mathematical problem. Both reading and writing rely heavily on the top three levels of Bloom's taxonomy (1956)—analysis, synthesis, and evaluation. Readers must analyze the information they read, then synthesize their prior knowledge with the new knowledge in the text, and finally judge whether or not the new knowledge is valid. Writers must analyze the information they gather, then synthesize the various pieces of information to create a unique chunk that communicates a new idea, and finally evaluate whether the information meets the readers' needs.

Let's look at a typical assignment in an introductory literature course.

Discuss how Updike's characterization of Sammy in "A&P" (his attitude, tone, perceptions, etc.,) influences the outcome of the story.

The assignment can be easily rephrased as a problem statement: What are the aspects of Updike's characterization of Sammy (his attitude, tone, perceptions, etc.) that influence the outcome of the story?

Before they can solve this problem, students need to solve the following intermediary problems.

1.   What are Sammy's attitudes toward his work? How does he perceive his work? How does the author let us know how Sammy feels about his work?

2.   What is my interpretation of the outcome of the story?

3.   What is the relationship between Sammy's attitude toward work and the story's outcome?

To solve this problem, readers must analyze Sammy's character. They must synthesize what they know about narrative devices from their prior knowledge with the devices the author uses to characterize Sammy, and finally they must evaluate whether these devices influence the story's outcome.

Now let's study a typical prompt for a first-year composition paper.

Newspapers and TV news shows are full of statistics on crime these days. The most alarming statistics have to do with young people. Overall crime rates are down, but the rate of violent crime committed by teens is up. Although polls show that crime is the number one concern of most Americans, people do not agree on how we should solve the problem. Some argue for more gun control, while others say we should build more prisons and lock up criminals for a longer time.

And so the debate—both written and spoken—continues, each side trying to state its position in a way that will convince the other side. Your assignment is to write an essay in which you add your voice to the on-going debate. Imagine that you're writing an Op Ed column in your local newspaper in response to the recent Editorial by Ernest van den Haag regarding the death penalty for juvenile murderers. Explain why you agree or disagree with van den Haag.

Once again, the assignment can be restated as a problem: How do I persuade my readers that van den Haag's ideas are or are not a good solution for reducing the number of juvenile murderers? As with the literature assignment, students will need to solve several intermediary problems before they can arrive at a solution. These include the following:

- What is my interpretation of van den Haag's editorial; what is he saying about juvenile murderers? What are van den Haag's arguments? How do I feel about van den Haag's ideas? How can I support or refute them?
- How will my readers' feel about van den Haag's ideas about juvenile murderers?
- What is the conventional style of an Op Ed column?
- What information should I include?
- How should I organize the information?
- What voice should I use?

In examining the problems posed by the two assignments, it becomes apparent that solutions will not come easily. The problems involved in reading the story and writing the editorial, as in reading and writing all texts, are "ill-defined" or "ill-structured"; there are no standard solutions, such as those in geometry or physics problems. Instead, each solution is unique to the individual working on the problem. Two people working on the same question will not arrive at the exact same conclusion. Yet, both may have acceptable responses. This is why teaching reading and writing is so difficult; we cannot simply give students a set of rules to follow. The five-paragraph theme may not be an appropriate organizational structure for a persuasive essay to a hostile reader. In fact, an effective persuasive essay may begin in a variety of ways, including a narrative written in the first person, a statement of the problem, or a recommendation for a solution to a problem, depending on the writer's previous knowledge and experience as well as on the readers' attitude toward the topic and the context in which the essay will be read, that is, the local newspaper, a professional journal, the Sunday supplement magazine, the Web.

Dealing with ill-defined problems can be especially difficult for working-class students. As we learned in Chapter 1, many of these students come from homes in which problems and issues are perceived as binomials; black and white, right and wrong. Their lives are governed by rules made by their parents; local, state, and national governments; the schools; their churches; their clubs; their work and their unions. They have had little experience in making their own decisions. Often faced with ill-structured problems, they become frustrated (McCall, 2000).

Because reading and writing texts involves solving ill-defined problems and because many students are not introduced to these problems in their homes, students need to learn the appropriate problem-solving strategies in the classroom. Much has already been written about teaching general problem solving (Bridges, 1992; Delisle, 1997; Flower, 1985; Marzano, 1991; Marzano, et al., 1988). We will not spend time discussing it in this book, but rather will focus on problem solving specifically in the English classroom.

To engage successfully in reading and writing then, students must learn not only the content of a course but also the strategies for solving the problems inherent in a course. Most of us, when we think of knowledge, consider only knowledge related to content (declarative knowledge). However, there is also knowledge related to the strategies required to acquire content knowledge (procedural knowledge) and the knowledge of when and where to use these strategies (conditional knowledge) (Marzano et al., 1988).

• *Declarative knowledge* is the knowledge we commonly think of when we refer to knowledge. It is the *what* of learning, consisting of episodic (knowledge of specific events) and semantic (general facts and word meanings) memory (Marzano et al., 1988). It is the content of a course; the concepts, facts, and data; the schemata related to organizational patterns and genres. Bloom's taxonomy (1956) is a taxonomy of declarative knowledge. As teachers, we are concerned with declarative knowledge when we write the goals and objectives in our lesson plans and when we develop tests for our courses. It is also the knowledge evaluated in the SATs and in state assessments. Much has already been written about the best methods for teaching declarative knowledge, based on our recognition that this information is stored in memory in associative chunks (Miller, 1956). We know that if students are provided with information that is related to general concepts or to information they have previously acquired, they will retain it better than if they are simply given lists of unrelated data (Caine and Caine, 1991).

• *Procedural* knowledge consists of heuristics used to acquire declarative knowledge. It is the *how* of learning and provides the rules for using the information stored in declarative memory. As teachers, we have become aware of the processes for learning to read and write over the past twenty years. But while we engage our students in these strategies, we seldom instruct them in when and why they should be used. Instead, we simply appropriate the strategies into our own lesson plans. Thus, we plan such activities as mapping, webbing, outlining, and chunking, but we usually do not require that students define each of these strategies, explain how and why each is used, or determine appropriate prewriting activities. Yet, it is this knowledge that they must have if they are to select an appropriate strategy that will enable them to engage successfully in a specific writing or reading task. The problem is that this knowledge often appears to be intuitive and automatic; we usually do not consciously recall it for our use. As you read this section of this chapter, you are predicting that the next paragraph will be concerned with the third type of knowledge listed in the paragraph preceding this list, without consciously thinking about using a prediction strategy based on our prior knowledge of the rule that a paragraph prior to a list should contain a forecast of the items to be listed. When we discuss the information in a textbook with our students, we often ask them, after reading the first paragraph in a section, "What do you predict you will read next?", but we do not ask them at the very beginning of the section before they have read anything, "What is the rule (what procedures do you need to follow) that will enable you to understand this section?" Nor do we ask them to differentiate between the procedures for understanding a poem and those for understanding a textbook. Yet, they must have this knowledge if they are to be able to comprehend various types of complex texts.

Heuristics are strategies for solving problems. Some, such as "Try to get the big picture before working on the details," are general and can be applied across content fields. Others, like "Analyze the audience when writing a workplace document," are domain specific; they relate only to specific content areas or subareas. *Procedural knowledge can be either general or domain (field) specific.*

A *domain* is characterized not only by a field of knowledge, such as literature, but also by the method of inquiry used to learn a specific body of knowledge. *A domain consists of semantic knowledge (knowledge of content) and procedural knowledge* (Adey and Shayer, 1993).

Figure 2–1

• *Conditional knowledge* relates to *when* and *where* the various rules in procedural knowledge should be applied. Some procedures can be used across content areas, such as "Vocabulary specific to a field must be learned in order a to read and write in that field." On the other hand, many procedures relate to a specific content area, such as reading, and cannot be applied to other areas, such as mathematics. Such strategies are *domain specific;* their use depends on the user's goals, the requirements of the problem, and the context in which the tasks must be performed (Weinstein and Meyer, 1991, p. 17). Students need to know which rules to apply under what conditions. In learning to write essays, students do not need to consider formatting a page, but in learning to write workplace documents, they need to study such aspects as typography, graphics, and page design. Recent research indicates that it is the domain-specific procedures that students need to acquire rather than the general procedures which we most often teach in order for them to engage successfully in problem-solving activities in their fields (Singley and Anderson, 1989).

Because students must be able to determine the procedures in which they need to engage as well as the conditions under which each procedure should be used if they are to acquire new content knowledge, the focus of learning to learn must be on the acquisition and selection of appropriate strategies. Furthermore, if students are to learn to transfer the knowledge they acquire in one English class to the next, they must learn not only the general strategies for learning to learn but also the heuristics that are domain specific and, thus, relate specifically to reading and writing texts.

Authentic Problem-Solving Tasks

To create situations in which students must consider strategies for solving literary and writing problems as well as recognize the conditions under which these strategies are valid, we need to develop authentic assignments that are presented in a problem, case-based format and that require higher order, critical thinking skills rather than the application of rules (Bruer, 1993, p. 220). Several versions of a task should be developed, so that over a period of time students have an opportunity to work on multiple variations, sometimes requiring the same, sometimes requiring different heuristics to engage successfully in the task.

For example, an assignment might involve developing a flyer aimed at getting parents to attend an upcoming PTA meeting. To engage in this task successfully, students need to determine arguments that will persuade parents to attend. Then they must determine the content, focus, organization, and style of the flyer in relation to the parents who will be reading the material. In solving this problem, students use strategies involved in writing persuasively that can be transferred to future assignments, such as writing a memo to their principal requesting a change in the cafeteria menu, or crafting a proposal to the Board of Education suggesting additional parking spaces, or composing an Op Ed column in the local newspaper responding to an editorial about students' failure to accept responsibility for their learning. Each of these follow-up assignments is for a different audience and a different purpose. Yet, each requires the student to analyze the audience and to make a decision about the content, focus, organization, and style of the text based on the results of their analysis. In addition, each requires that they consider arguments that support their stance, that they consider arguments that their opponents might use against their proposal, and that they consider arguments that preempt those of their readers by refuting them. By engaging in several tasks, such as those cited here, that differ in some aspects but are analogous in the kinds of strategies required to solve them, students can begin to acquire conditional knowledge, thereby recognizing when and how to transfer the procedural knowledge they are acquiring (Jones, 1987). In this case, the procedural and conditional knowledge the students acquire is domain specific and directly related to the declarative knowledge of the domain—persuasive writing.

To make this assignment truly authentic, students should design the flyer for an actual upcoming PTA meeting with their flyers actually distributed to parents. The other projects could be handled similarly. The principal and cook for the school might be invited to the class where they are presented with the proposal to change the menu; a member of the Board of Education might be invited to class to receive the proposal for additional parking; the Op Ed column could actually be sent to the local newspaper for publication. Thus, by engaging students in authentic tasks that involve problems in reading and writing, students acquire not only declarative knowledge but also procedural and conditional knowledge for solving analogous types of literacy problems that they can transfer from one project to the next.

Mary Yorke, who teaches seniors at Munster High School, in Munster, Indiana, has been involving her students in Problem-Based Learning in her English class for the past ten years. "Problem-based learning is worth every challenge it presents, " Mary comments. "What greater goal is there for educators than to teach their students to become thinkers."

Each year, the class is assigned to research a problem faced by a company. Students must select the business they want to work with and then write a letter requesting information about the company's problems and offering to assist in finding solutions. Students are urged to select three companies, so that if two fail to respond or provide a problem, students still have one that meets their needs.

Mary, who had been teaching for about twenty years before instituting this feature in her classroom, comments, "It's the first time I really felt students understood what it meant to write for a reader." She has been using the activity ever since.

Mary's success with the method surpassed anything she ever imagined. In 1998, to fulfill the assignment, one of her students, Dana Brzozkiewicz, wrote to Exxon Corporation, along with two other companies—Nordstrom's and Fannie May. Exxon responded by asking for help in solving the problem of the tiger. Since the oil spill of 1989 off the coast of Alaska by one of its ships, the Valdez, Exxon had been trying to overcome its image as an environmental despoiler. One of the ways it had been attempting to build a new image had been by becoming involved in environmental issues. Aware that its logo for over 100 years, the tiger, was becoming extinct in its natural habitat, the company began a campaign to help preserve the tiger. Dana researched the problem and submitted a solution. Exxon was so pleased with her recommendations that they invited her to attend the Year of the Tiger Conference they were sponsoring along with the National Fish and Wildlife Foundation in Dallas, Texas. More than 130 experts from 18 countries attended the conference in an effort to develop a plan that would enable the tiger to continue to survive. At the conference banquet, Exxon CEO Lee Raymond presented Dana with a Save the Tiger plaque and the first Habitats: Realm of the Tiger educational kit, developed by Exxon and the National Geographic Society.

Mary explains her unit below.

Teaching a Problem-Based Research Paper

Mary Yorke, Munster High School

Before students can write, they must know how to think. Too often we tell our students "Think about what you are saying." But what does it mean "to think?" And how can we teach our students to become engaged in this process?

Problem-based learning gave me a way to teach my students to become independent thinkers. This method is not another educational buzz word that will go the way of other "educational gimmicks." It is a viable technique for reaching students from kindergarten through college and on to medical and dental schools.

I begin by creating a problem that will entice my students into wanting to find a solution as well as provide them with the opportunity to learn necessary writing skills. I try to select problems in which my students have a personal interest. For example, one of my most successful topics related to the summer reading program required at our high school. The students received the following prompt.

> You are the principal of the high school and the school board wants you to define the pros and cons of the high school's summer reading program so it can decide whether or not the program should be continued. You will be expected to give a presentation to the school board at its next meeting.
>
> *Background:* The high school presently conducts a summer reading program which requires that every student read three books from an assigned list. The students must then take a computerized test that covers the books they read. The grades for the test count as twenty-five per cent of the grade for the first six weeks of the fall term.

The first step in the learning process is to carefully establish the parameters of the problem. Too often students do not think through all of the ramifications of a topic. We begin the first step with brainstorming. As the teacher, I too often am tempted to expound on the topic the students need to research; remaining silent while the students stare at me is uncomfortable. However, silence is a catalyst for forcing them to start thinking. In this student-centered, high-interest environment, everyone is encouraged to proffer some ideas. I write all their ideas on poster board. We sometimes spend two days learning how to think through what a sound investigation would require, considering such questions as "What does a summer reading program do for the students at MHS?" "Are the parents behind the program?" "How do the teachers and administrators feel about the program?" "Are the tests fair?" "Do other schools have such programs?" What happens to the students' grades because of the testing?" "How many students read the books?" "How many watch the video?" Are the books good choices for 21st century teenagers?"

All students are then assigned an area to research. At this point the students identify the information on their area of the topic that they already know and then they establish everything they think they need to learn to solve the problem. Their grades are based on the depth of the information they gather. Students are allowed to work in groups of two or three if the topic area needs considerable research.

The joy of this type of learning is that mini-lessons, such as "How to handle computer research," "How to interview someone," "How to ask unbiased questions," can be incorporated into each problem. The possibilities for lessons are endless.

The next step is for the students to gather their information. Once they have their data, they need to duplicate enough copies for everyone in class, so that the entire class can analyze the material they will be using. Realizing that some sources may not be credible is a valuable life lesson. After I have taken the students through the process of gathering information in order to solve a problem, they are ready to draft their presentation.

From this kind of personalized essay, students move on to the research paper and now it is time for them to go through the process of solving a problem on their own [thus engaging in forward- and backward-reaching transfer]. Students are required to select three companies with which they might be interested in working. They then write a letter to each company asking if they can work on solving a problem the company faces. [It was for this assignment that Dana Brzozkiewicz worked with Exxon on the problem of the extinction of tigers.]

During this unit I include a mini-lesson on writing a formal business letter so that the students' letters appear professionally written. Throughout the remainder of the project, I provide mini-lessons on writing a research paper; citing sources; finding sources, including those on the internet; evaluating internet and other sources for validity; and using other electronic media in addition to the Internet to locate information.

Tips for Developing Successful Problems

A. Determining the Subject (Problem)
    1. Decide the curricular goals to be met and/or the subject matter to be covered.
    2. The subject matter should be related to real life and the way the world works.
    3. The subject matter should be related to your students' world or their immediate lives.
    4. Determine the length of time you have to spend on the activity.
    5. Create roles for your students that are realistic and meaningful.

B. Using Resources
    1. Try to have the following resources available for students.
        - Speakers/experts for personal or telephone interviews or presentations
        - Written materials in the form of books, magazines, etc.
        - Internet sites
    2. The more experts students talk to, the more real the problem becomes, and the more the students will care.

C. Criteria for Good Problems
    1. There is no simple right or wrong solution.
    2. The problems are within the students' world.
    3. The problems are interesting to adolescents.
    4. The problems are interdisciplinary.
    5. The problems have multiple levels of concern.
    6. The problems allow your students to demonstrate their knowledge to a real audience.

Tips for Developing Successful Problems *Adapted from Krynock/Robb, 1994.*

Strategies for Learning to Learn

Learning to learn consists of the following three interrelated aspects, all of which are required if learning is to take place.

- *Transfer of knowledge.* The appropriate knowledges that have been learned in prior tasks must be transferred to learning new tasks. Transfer involves metacognition, cognitive flexibility, and analogical reasoning.

- *Critical/higher order, inquiry-based thinking.* Learners must engage in deep/critical, inquiry-based, cognitive processes in order to recognize the abstract aspects of a problem and thus apply appropriate strategies from previous cases to new cases.

- *Appropriate attitudes.* Learners must assume a "disposition to expend effort to learn" that involves persistence and assume the responsibility for their own learning (Halpern, 1998).

Transfer of Knowledge

Transfer of knowledge is "the ability to learn in one situation and then to use that learning, possibly in modified or generalized form in other situations where it is appropriate" (Hunter, 1971, p. 2). Recognize transfer of learning as the goal for all school instruction: Hunter perceives this skill as the "heart and core of problem solving, creative thinking and all other higher mental processes (2). . . . The ability to transfer past learning which is appropriate to a present situation is one of the most critical factors in perception, insight, reasoning and originality (1)." Halpern (1998) provides a more practical view, perceiving transfer of learning as essential if students are to succeed in a world in which technology is creating a constantly changing environment. "The goal of instruction designed to help students become better thinkers is transferability to real-world, out-of-the-classroom situations." (451)

Transfer occurs along two paths: the "low road" and the "high road" (Salomon and Perkins, 1989). Low-road transfer occurs unconsciously. Based on extended practice with many similar tasks, it results in automaticity, a stimulus-controlled response. Many of our daily tasks, such as reading, writing, and driving a car, are carried out automatically, without thinking about the various steps involved. When we type, our fingers fly over the keyboard hitting the correct keys without our thinking, "I need to hit an 'R' which is located in the top left row." In fact, if we are asked where the 'R' is located on the typewriter, most of us have to pause to think about it. When we are about to read a journal article, we do not consciously think "I need to engage in prereading. This is a journal article so I expect it to be written in academic style, to be concerned with education and to help me learn to teach better. The title will provide me with an idea of the article's focus, the introduction will forecast the various aspects of the article I will read about and the headings in the article will tell me when I am about to read each of those aspects." Yet, this is exactly what we do. We are simply not conscious of doing it.

The second type of transfer, "high-road transfer," is based on conscious, learned behavior. It is the result of a conscious decision to use a specific procedure to solve a specific problem. When a student is consistently late for a class, we consciously consider a number of potential solutions to the problem and select the one that seems most appropriate. We may have learned the solutions in a course on classroom management, or we may have learned them informally by inferring them from listening to colleagues talk about procedures they used to solve a similar problem, or we may have read them in a journal article. Regardless of whether we learned the solutions formally or informally, we recognize that there is a potential for using them again, and so we internalize them in our long-term memory where we can retrieve them when we need them. This is called "forward-reaching transfer" (Schoenfeld, 1979). It involves recognizing that strategies we have just used to solve one problem can be used to solve other future problems (Salomon and Perkins, 1989). This recognition causes the brain to store the strategies in the chunks of our memory that are related to those future problems, thus enabling us to locate them when we need them which is "backward-reaching" transfer. Faced with a new problem, we search our memories for knowledge that might help us solve it. If that knowledge was stored through forward-reaching transfer, then we should be able to retrieve it.

During the first assignment in Tim's Documentation Writing Course, I engaged the class in forward-reaching transfer, requiring them to think about how they might use the strategies they had learned in future assignments. Tim then used backward-reaching transfer when he was faced with the second assignment. He thought about what he had done previously to decide how to approach the new assignment and was able to remember the appropriate strategies from the first lesson.

Because the best chance for people to recall appropriate strategies for solving a problem is based on their ability to "foresee a large range of the possible situations in which a problem they have just solved might be useful," there is a direct relationship between encoding procedures and retrieval procedures (Kolodner, 1997, p. 61). The greater the number of connections to information stored in memory, the greater the likelihood that the appropriate solution will be recalled (Halpern, 1998, p. 453). It is the ability of "intelligent novices" to use forward-reaching high-road transfer that enables them to retrieve appropriate processes for acquiring new skills or learning new knowledge more quickly than others. The key is that the processes have been consciously learned and stored. Because low-road transfer is done without conscious recognition of how it can be used in the future, it cannot be retrieved easily.

For some of us, transferring the procedures we used for one task to solve a new task seems obvious. We may have learned this concept through either formal or informal instruction, or we may have simply intuited it. It was through intuition that Tim recognized he could transfer the procedures from the first project to the next. However, although our students engage in low-road transfer after sufficient practice in a skill, few engage in high-road transfer. One of the major reasons for their failure is that they perceive the content knowledge they learn in school as independent bits of information rather than as parts of larger related constructs and schema. They perceive a sonnet as different from a limerick and file each of these subgenres in their memory as separate entities, without recognizing that the procedures for comprehending both are analogous. Thus, they fail to build bridges that relate their prior knowledge to new learning tasks. Yet, without these bridges, they cannot transfer knowledge across domains (Adey and Shayer 1993).

This inability to recognize relationships among bits of information is often carried into the workplace. In a workshop I provided at a nuclear power plant, I was asked to provide a segment on writing letters recommending changes in procedures being proposed for the industry after completing a segment on writing letters requesting a change in plant-specific procedures. The nuclear engineers with whom I was working did not recognize what Tim had discovered: that the basic heuristics for writing workplace correspondence are the same. Regardless of whether it is a letter of request or a recommendation letter, they must analyze the audience, purpose, and context for the document in order to determine the focus, content, organization, style, and format of the document. Thus, for students to transfer information, they must recognize that the content information they are acquiring is part of a large chunk of knowledge and that the procedures they are using to carry out their tasks and the conditions under which those tasks are conducted are an integral part of that knowledge.

To become aware of the procedures they are using to accomplish a task or solve a problem, students need to engage in metacognition and analogical reasoning, and they must maintain cognitive flexibility.

Metacognition. Metacognition is the act of thinking about thinking. It is central to students' being able to transfer their knowledge from one assignment to another, from one course to another. If our students are to learn to transfer knowledge, then they must become aware of the processes they use and the value of using them so that they can retrieve them at appropriate times from their long-term memory and use them to learn new tasks. We can help our students acquire these aspects of procedural and conditional knowledge, respectively, by engaging them in metacognitive activities that create both an awareness of the processes and a recognition of their value in solving specific reading and writing problems.

Metacognition requires that students take time to reflect on the declarative knowledge they have gained and the procedural and conditional knowledge they have used to learn a content area. "The processes that have recently earned the title metacognitive are central to learning and development. . . . Some form of self awareness . . . is critical for any efficient problem-solving system" (Brown, 1987, pp. 65, 79). By gaining awareness of what they do and the strategies they use, students can begin to internalize the procedural skills they are acquiring, which is the process Pressley, Snyder, and Cariglia-Bull (1987) found in good strategy users. When students internalize problem-solving heuristics, they learn not only "how to get a particular task done independently but also how to set about learning new problems. In other words, the child learns how to learn (Brown, 1987, p. 109) and is able to transfer that learning from one task to the next. Thus, we need to help our students not only acquire procedural and conditional knowledge in reading and writing but also internalize these procedures, so that they can increasingly assume responsibility for using them to solve problems on their own.

Flavell (1976) perceives metacognition involving two aspects: (1) "one's knowledge concerning one's own cognitive processes and products" and (2) "the active monitoring and consequent regulation and orchestration of these processes in relation to . . . some concrete goal or objective" (232). Thus, metacognition involves not only thinking about thinking but also using the knowledge you derived for acquiring new knowledge.

By engaging in metacognition, students can acquire three types of knowledge (Garofalo, 1986).

1. *Knowledge of themselves as problem solvers.* Through metacognition students can discover that they are successful in interpreting texts when they reread them at least once or they often arrive at their thesis statement at the end of writing their essay.

2. *Knowledge of how they deal with the scope, demands, and requirements of a task.* Through metacognition, students can recognize that when they have gathered a great deal of information, they want to include all of it in their texts; or that when they are assigned to read a play, they prefer to see it on a tape; or that they have difficulty understanding poetry, because the syntax doesn't follow traditional grammatical patterns for English.

3. *Knowledge of the heuristics for solving a task* (Garafalo, 1986). Through metacognition, they can discover that by reconstructing a line of poetry so that it follows a traditional syntactic pattern, they can begin to understand it; or that by placing related pieces of information together in chunks, they can begin to organize a report.

Students need to engage in metacognitive activities in order to achieve forward- and backward-reaching transfer. Thus, they need to be willing to take the time at the conclusion of a lesson, to reflect on the strategies they have just used, and to consider how they might use these same strategies in solving future problems. They also need to take time during prewriting or prereading to reflect on previous tasks that might be analogous to the one on which they are working and to consider whether the procedural knowledge they used to complete the previous task could be used to solve this one.

At the conclusion of the problem-solving activity on creating the flyer that we discussed earlier, students should be asked to reflect on the strategies they used to determine the organization, style, and format of the flyer and to determine the focus and content that would most likely influence the parents to attend the meeting. Furthermore, they should be involved in reflecting on how they might use these strategies in future assignments. Such reflections could assume several forms:

- A class discussion
- Small group discussions with each group reporting back to the whole group
- A journal entry
- An analytical report or essay for their peers
- Instructions to their peers for writing persuasive documents

When a new task, such as to write a memo to the principal requesting more student parking spaces, is introduced, students should be asked to reflect on previous tasks that are analogous to the one they are about to work on. Their reflection should trigger a recognition that the task to develop the PTA flyer is similar to the new one in relation to its general purpose—to persuade readers to do something—although the two assignments differ in terms of the type of document and the specific audience and purpose. Students should then reflect on the strategies they used to solve the previous problem—how to persuade the reader to do what the writer wants and how to determine the content, focus, style, and organization—to determine whether or not the strategies used previously can be used to help solve the problems associated with the present task. Once again students should recognize that the strategies for writing persuasively and determining content, etc., are relevant to both tasks. At the end of this activity, while engaging in metacognition, students can expand their repertoire of strategies to include the following ones.

- Consider previous tasks to determine analogous ones
- Consider the analogous aspects of similar tasks
- Consider whether the strategies used for the previous analogous tasks can be used for the present task

A major difficulty inherent in this method is that students may not have had prior experience with similar problems or they may not have learned strategies to help them find the solutions to analogous problems. In either case, it is incumbent on us to help students learn these strategies. If these are taught as students encounter a problem, there is a much greater chance that students will learn them because they will be able to hook them to an actual problem.

Chad Bush who teaches at Crown Point High School uses reflection in his classes to help students' learn to understand the relationship between themselves, their writing, the literature they read, and the world around them. When Chad first began teaching several years ago, he realized that his students' writing was "technically satisfactory," but "uninvolved," and therefore "uninteresting" and "flat." Their analysis of the literature they were studying was also "uninvolved"; they made no connection between the characters and themes in the works they read and the world around them. To try to engage students in more in-depth learning, he introduced a daily reflective activity at the end of each class. For some of his students, especially those who came from a culture that stressed privacy, keeping emotions in check and maintaining an outer air of calm was difficult, because it required that they recognize their deepest emotions, use these to give life to the characters and ideas they developed in their writings, and understand the characters and ideas of the texts they were reading. For others, whose culture was an overt, emotional one, these activities provided an outlet that they seldom had in a school setting. Over time, both groups learned to share and were able to grow in their ability to write essays, short stories, and poems and in their ability to analyze the literature they read.

Chad explains the ways he uses reflection in the following description.

Reflecting on the Relationship Between Self and the World Through Literature and Writing

Chad Bush, Crown Point High School

Reflection is understanding self in relationship to understanding the world around you. I begin validating reflection in the classroom on the first day. Students are asked to brainstorm their most important learning experiences. I facilitate ideas by suggesting that learning takes place everywhere, not just in school. It is a twenty-minute opening-day activity that levels the playing field and gives a group of individuals insight into the lives of others. I reflect with my students, always!

Reflection involves the following three relationships.

1. The relationship between our lives and experiences with the material we've covered

2. The way in which the techniques we have used and come to understand can be applied to our lives

3. The relationship between techniques of communication and the material we've covered

The means of reflection vary with each writing assignment. I may ask students to reflect as part of a group discussion, or I may ask them to place their reflections in a journal entry, or I may even assign them to show their reflections as a piece of reflective artwork. When they see a relationship between themselves and what they have been learning, their ideas come pouring out. I often learn in these sessions. Not everyone shares all the time. That's okay, and I tell them that. Reflection is an internal process and sometimes it needs to remain personal.

I don't know whether or not students become more self-aware in one semester. I do know that high school is a definitive time for development of the social self. High school is a time of clicks and groups and students need to fit in somewhere, from this point in their lives on. So learning to understand self and others through reflection is important. I would say students articulate their views of themselves sharply by semester's end. And, their ability to share insights that they may have previously had but couldn't share, or never had before, helps not only the individual but also everyone in the group. Students leave my room better writers, better readers, and more in touch with themselves as people.

Susan, a Japanese-American student, was one of those I watched grow as the semester progressed. She was a 2.8 GPA student enrolled in "average tracked" academic courses. She took my creative writing class because, as she told the class during our introductory session, her parents insisted that she not waste time with a study hall. She insisted that she wrote well. Her intelligence was evident, but she saw education as a means to an end. She saw no value in the process or life-journey of learning.

I began the semester with a reflective discussion of a human emotion. For Susan's class I had chosen "sorrow." The class gathered in a circle on the floor. I began this first session by asking the students to express the emotion of sorrow through facial and body language. This set a tone for the class so that the students could move on to discussing their own encounters with sorrow. Students shared personal moments and the effect of these moments on their lives. I read a eulogy that I had given at the funeral of a student. We read "Shaving" by Leslie Norris, and then we wrote memoirs of these moments. I wrote along with the students as I always do. Most students wrote from their personal experiences, but Susan made hers up. It was obvious when the students shared their stories by reading them aloud. Susan expressed little emotion and understood none of her "moment." When the other students responded to her memoir with questions, she couldn't answer them.

Susan continued to participate in the various daily reflective activities at the surface level. But it became obvious during the self-evaluation exercise I require students to engage in at the end of the first six weeks that she had been undergoing some deep changes. Susan evaluated her own writing as insincere and not genuine. She gave her memoir the grade of D+, commenting, with a great deal of new insight, "I am skilled at writing techniques, but I need to be told what to think about."

As the semester passed, Susan's work improved. She began to incorporate nuances of depth in her work. Her participation grew more insightful, and her presence helped others reflect successfully on their own learning.

Susan's work revolved around two issues: her Japanese heritage and her Catholic religion. The effect of these two aspects of her character on her response to reading and writing became evident during the final assignment.

As a culminating exercise, students create a portfolio of their writings. The portfolio itself is a box designed to reflect the students' reflection of themselves as writers. During the final period, students resumed their reflection circles on the floor, shared their boxes, and read two of their pieces.

When it was Susan's turn, she showed us a design of a lampshade turned upside down. She had created a base for it that she had painted a bright red. On this base sat a simple chair made of toothpicks. On one side of the shade hung a blank white cardboard movie screen. Behind the screen were Susan's writings. Susan explained that the world outside the shade is red, full of danger and challenge. Until now she had been confined, by her own insecurities, to the chair, watching her life on the screen. She explained how her Japanese heritage and her Catholic faith had created barriers that inhibited her full participation in exploring life.

Susan had learned to reflect on the relationship between her own world and the world around her and, in so doing, had found a bit of herself.

Analogical Reasoning. To successfully transfer knowledge from one task to another, students need to recognize the similarities and differences between tasks. "Analogy is a clever, sophisticated process used in creative discovery. . . . It is a device for conveying that two situations or domains share relational structure despite arbitrary degrees of difference in the objects that make up the domains. Common relations are essential to analogy: common objects are not" (Gentner and Markman, 1997, p. 45).

Students have been required to engage in analogical reasoning throughout their schooling as they have studied the use of metaphors in literature. A metaphor is a form of analog; it indicates similarities between one or more features of two often dissimilar objects. To understand a metaphor, readers must recognize the features of the objects on which the author is focusing and then identify the aspects of those features that the author perceives as similar. When Romeo cries, "But, soft! What light through yonder window breaks?/It is the east, and Juliet is the sun," Shakespeare is not comparing such concrete aspects as the color of the sun, the heat emanating from the sun, or the shape of the sun to Juliet, but rather the abstract concept of radiance.

The problem encountered by most people, regardless of whether they are interpreting a metaphor or transferring information, is in recognizing the analogous features. In transferring knowledge, people often have difficulty differentiating between those aspects that directly affect a solution and those that do not (Bassok, 1990; Novick, 1988). It is this lack of understanding that was the cause of the engineers' failure to recognize that writing a letter of recommendation would follow the same procedures as writing a letter of request. Rather than focusing on the similarities in the procedural knowledge required to complete the task, they focused on the differences between the purposes for the letters and the conventions of the two subgenres. When the features of two tasks are similar, that is, the second task might have been a letter of recommendation *but* to a different person and about a different topic, people can more easily solve a problem, but when these features differ, novice problem solvers, such as our students, have far more difficulty recognizing which previous procedures are appropriate for solving a new task (Hammond, et al., 1991; Novick, 1998).

Another problem with analogical transfer is that many people have a tendency to generalize a procedure; they want to use it for many similar tasks without realizing that critical aspects of these tasks are not analogous. Most of the writing the engineers do in college is related to lab reports. The conventional organizational structure for a lab report requires that events be recorded in chronological order. Because engineers are familiar with using this organizational pattern, they often apply it to any document they write, without recognizing that in some situations the structure is inappropriate. For example, in a proposal, when readers are already familiar with a problem, there is no need to give a chronological history of it. Engineers at one of Tennessee Valley Authority's (TVA) nuclear utility plants misapplied this chronological structure to a letter to the Nuclear Regulatory Commission requesting a reduction in a fine that had been levied against the utility for failing to fix a problem in "a timely manner." Guidelines indicated that for a utility to obtain a reduction, it needed to prove that it had done all it could to solve the problem for which it was being fined. However, instead of beginning the letter with a list of the utility's efforts to solve the problem, the engineers at TVA began with a chronological narrative of everything that had gone wrong, thus reinforcing readers' perceptions of the utility's inefficiency in solving the problems. The engineers used an inappropriate organizational pattern because they failed to recognize that the purpose of their document was not analogous to that of a lab report and that therefore a different organizational structure needed to be applied.

In these cases, the engineers were applying backward-reaching transfer, but the analogies were inappropriate. Thus, students need to learn to identify the appropriate features. To help them, they need to be involved in case-based or problem-solving activities that allow them to work on a variety of tasks with both similar and dissimilar aspects.

Cognitive Flexibility.   To engage successfully in analogical reasoning, students need to be open minded, ready to change their minds as they compare problems. The ability to recognize differences in relatively similar problems and to understand that these differences may require different procedures for finding a solution or to recognize similarities in what appear to be dissimilar tasks and to determine the appropriateness of using previous procedures for completing these tasks successfully is called cognitive flexibility (Spiro et al., 1988). Students need to recognize that a direct correlation does not always exist between a strategy and a solution. Rather real-world situations are "messy," and a strategy they used to solve one problem may not solve the next because the context for the new one differs from that of the previous one. Students must have experience working on numerous complex and ill-structured problems that require different strategies. "When students are not given this opportunity, they tend to consider situations superficially, oversimplify the problems presented, and rely on solutions that do not encompass all of the multiple and interrelated aspects (Spiro et al., 1988, p. 378). This surface thinking can often be seen in the themes students write for freshman composition and in their responses to a literary work.

Students need to work on as wide a variety of tasks as possible so that they can build a repertoire of strategies for solving problems that are similar in some aspects and different in others. Furthermore, they need to become comfortable working on complex, ill-structured situations similar to ones found in the world of the academy.

Jim McCall, who teaches English at Valparaiso High School, helps students learn to read literature as a problem-solving project by drawing a comparison between literary analysis and detective work. Through a unit on the detective novel as a genre, he demonstrates how clues that lead to the solution of a mystery story are analogous to the clues found in texts that help readers analyze a work of fiction. According to Jim, "Having students develop their deductive reasoning as well as defend their logic provides a natural bridge to text analysis and quotation support."

Jim describes his unit in the following section.

Teaching Deductive Reasoning To Learn Literary Analysis

Jim McCall, Valparaiso High School

The maxim of education has always been "prepare the students for their most important classroom: life." We need to teach students not what to think, but *how* to think. Deductive reasoning gives students a solid foundation on which to build higher level cognitive skills.

Deductive reasoning is the dissection of data to produce a logical conclusion. Quite simply, it is the ability to think rationally in a given situation. The following lesson is part of the introductory unit for teaching deductive reasoning. The lesson assumes the form of a Look–Learn–Do pedagogy and is based on the reading/writing connection.

Students are first introduced to the concept of deductive reasoning. They then read several detective stories. I use this subgenre because the solutions are based on deductive reasoning. Integrated into these readings are mini-lessons on the structure and conventions of this subgenre in particular and on the short story genre in general. Eventually students compose their own short detective story. Finally, they reflect on the process and consider how they can use the strategies they employed, deductive reasoning specifically, in other contexts such as literary analysis [forward-reaching transfer].

On the first day of the unit, I read a children's detective story to the class and ask them to solve the mystery as we go along. The *Encyclopedia Brown* series by Donald J. Sobol is an excellent aid for this activity. We discuss how the detective arrives at the solution and then I ask the students to use metacognition as they go step by step through their own thought processes and discuss how they arrived at their conclusions. After the class discussion, I read another mystery and ask the students to solve it as we go along. This second story provides an opportunity for them to recognize that they can use the strategies they used previously in a similar instance [backward-reaching transfer]. However, I alter the instance to some degree. This time, the students are required to write down the clues that helped them arrive at their conclusions as well as the connection between the clues and their conclusions. This twofold exercise in metacognition serves as a means of transfer and helps the class become more self-aware throughout the rest of the unit.

In the next activity in the unit, students execute and hone their deductive reasoning while writing a short story. Students assume the role of police detectives, create a short story, and defend their findings by analyzing and explaining their thought processes.

The first day of the project is devoted to the "prewriting" step in the writing process. A table is set up at the front of the room and on it are six to twelve common items (battery, golf tee, parking permit, bus schedule, matches, a phone number) as well as some not-so-obvious items (computer cable, bicycle spoke, etc.—creativity with these objects is crucial). I then explain to the students that they are police detectives and I provide them with a scenario. While on duty, they find a body with the objects on the front table on it. Their job is to identify the different objects and to hypothesize the use of each by the dead person.

The class must then create a character profile that is based on the evidence found on the dead person. This profile should include gender, approximate age, occupation, hobbies, marital status, and habits.

Next, the students develop a chronological outline of the person's last day, based on the objects found. Students are expected to adhere to the conventions and structure of the short detective story.

In the next phase the students synthesize, revise, and publish their short stories. The students compose their short stories by following their outlines and expanding the details of the events. When this stage is finished, the students are separated into groups of three and are given "peer revision guides" that allow them to focus on specific aspects (detail, logic, structure) of each others' stories. After they revise, the stories are ready to be published. Publication in this case means the stories are read aloud to the class at which time the class scrutinizes the logic the writer uses to solve the mystery. The class's questions of "why?" force the author to defend his deductive reasoning and reinforces the importance of logic.

This activity provides a bridge to literary analysis. It helps to cut down on our own explanations of when to quote material from a text in a research paper. Using backward-reaching transfer, I draw analogies between the deductive reasoning used to solve a mystery and that used to understand literature. Furthermore I point out the similarities between clues in a detective novel and textual cues in a literary work. I also demonstrate how citations in a literary analysis help readers understand a writer's logic in arriving at a certain interpretation. Students begin to realize logic dictates cause/effect relationships and they are better able to defend their interpretations of literature.

These results are also relevant beyond the English classroom. I was once approached by a history teacher who complained that one of my students had disrupted his lecture by asking "Why did the Black Hand assassinate Prince Ferdinand?" instead of just accepting the fact as a cause of World War I.

Whether it is in the classroom or out in life, students who know how to think and can defend their views with logic are destined to not only succeed in life, but excel as well.

Tips for Teaching Reasoning

A. Standards: Students' work should demonstrate the following traits.
    - Clarity
    - Specificity
    - Relevance
    - Logical inferences and deductions
    - Accuracy
    - Consistency
    - Depth
    - Completeness

B. Strategies: Students should learn to engage in the following.
    - Evaluating evidence
    - Analyzing issues, problems, beliefs, actions, arguments, interpretations
    - Questioning deeply
    - Exploring significant similarities and differences
    - Exploring and evaluating solutions

Critical/ Higher Order/Inquiry-Based Thinking

Because reading and writing are problem-solving activities, students need to use critical, higher order, inquiry-based thinking. Critical thinking, according to Halpern (1998), is "purposeful, reasoned, and goal-directed" (450). It involves "formulating inferences, calculating likelihoods, and making decisions . . . . When people think critically, they are evaluating the outcomes of their thought processes—how good a decision is or how well a problem is solved." Thus, critical thinking involves "evaluation or judgment, ideally with the goal of providing useful and accurate feedback" (451). To engage in critical thinking then we must function at the higher levels of Bloom's taxonomy—analysis, synthesis, and evaluation. In addition, Halpern (1998) suggests we cannot engage in these levels in a rote or mechanical manner, but rather we need to be "reflective, sensitive to the context, and self-monitoring" (451). In other words, to engage in higher order, critical thinking skills requires skill in metacognition. Halpern suggests the following taxonomy of critical thinking skills that students need to master in order to succeed at the kinds of tasks they will encounter in college: verbal reasoning, argument analysis, hypothesis testing, probability, and generation, evaluation, and selection of alternatives. Brown (1996) extends the concept of cognitive thinking to include the willingness to doubt. He indicates that students need to learn to question evidence and authority and that they must engage in their courses with a critical approach to what is being taught.

Certainly Tim used higher order thinking skills when he synthesized the prior knowledge related to users that he had gained from a usability test he had conducted for a previous project with the decision he needed to make regarding optional methods for users to enter data. Furthermore, he was obviously engaging in critical thinking when he not only generated alternative presentations but also evaluated the consequences of each.

Literature and composition assignments that students encounter at the college level, such as the one in which Tim was engaged, require higher order cognitive skills. However, we seldom provide our students with instruction in these skills, especially as they relate to reading and writing. Yet teachers at the college level expect that students have already learned the heuristics involved and can engage in the higher order, inquiry-based, cognitive processes required.

Let's look again at the two assignments on p.27-28 that are typical of assignments given to first-year students in literature and composition, respectively, and consider the various skills and strategies students need to have acquired to succeed in responding to them.

To succeed in writing the paper for the literature course, students will need to engage in the following higher order cognitive skills.

Analysis. Students need to analyze the main character's traits, the traits of the girls that are unacceptable to the store manager, Sammy's attitude toward the girls, the manager's attitude toward the girls, the girls' attitude toward Sammy, and the other shoppers' attitudes toward the girls. They also have to analyze the narrative devices the author uses to characterize Sammy, including description, dialog, background information, etc.

Synthesis. Students have to synthesize their own prior experience of society's view of improper dress with society's view in the middle of the twentieth century. They also have to synthesize the various aspects of Sammy's character to develop a portrait of Sammy, and they have to synthesize the author's characterization of Sammy with the story's conclusion.

Evaluation. Students need to evaluate whether Updike's characterization of Sammy is sufficient for readers to accept the story's outcome.

Critical skills. Students need to examine Updike's *verbal cues* as they relate to Sammy's narrative tone in order to deduce his view of the girls, the manager, the ethics of his society. They need to *test* their *hypothesis* that Updike's characterization either supported or failed to support the outcome of the story, and they need to *generate* and then *evaluate* alternative endings.

Inquiry skills. Students need to approach the entire task with a willingness to doubt the skill of the author, questioning whether or not Updike's characterization is sufficient to warrant the conclusion.

Now let's look at the prompt for the composition and consider the higher order skills required to complete it.

Analysis. Students need to analyze van den Haag's arguments for reducing the number of juvenile murderers, and they need to analyze arguments in other articles they read about the same topic. They also need to analyze their own arguments for or against the topic.

Synthesis. Students need to synthesize the arguments from the various sources. They also need to synthesize their own arguments with the arguments they are reading. Finally they need to synthesize all of their ideas to create a unifying organizing idea or thesis statement.

Evaluation. Students need to evaluate each of the arguments they read as well as their own arguments to determine the validity of each.

Critical skills. Students need to use *verbal reasoning* to persuade their readers to accept their argument. They also need to *test* van den Haag's *hypothesis* to determine whether they agree or disagree with it. If they disagree with it, they will need *to generate, evaluate,* and *select* alternative hypotheses.

Inquiry skills. Students need to approach the topic with a questioning mind, examining with skepticism each of the arguments presented.

Many of our students fail to engage in the kind of dialog required by these prompts, because they do not know how to do so. Instead, they respond with what Stanovich (1994) terms "dysrationalia," "thinking and behavior that is significantly below the level of the individual's intellectual capacity," (11), and what Langer calls "mindlessness," "the shallow processing of information that allows outrageous anomalies to pass unnoticed" (cited in Perkins and Grotzer, 1997, p. 1125)

Perkins categorizes the kind of thinking that many students display as follows.

- *Hasty.* Impulsive, insufficient investment in deep processing and examining of alternatives
- *Narrow.* Failing to challenge assumptions, examine other points of view
- *Fuzzy.* Careless, imprecise
- *Sprawling.* Generally disorganized and unfocused

Once again the reasons for these kinds of responses are related to both students' culture and their school environment. A culture that establishes parents as the source of all decisions eliminates the need for students to think through problems, and a culture that inculcates unquestioning acceptance of statements made by such authority figures as parents, teachers, and clergy prevents students from learning to examine the assumptions underlying the various ideas put forth. Furthermore, if students are not able to observe parents or teachers engaged in "deep thinking," then they have no models on which to base their own problem-solving cognitive behavior. And we have already discussed the results of classrooms in which the teachers provide the answers to questions. In fact, teachers seldom provide students with sufficient time to consider questions that require deep thinking.

To overcome Langer's "mindless" thinking, students need to learn strategies for engaging in deep thinking. Furthermore they need to learn to question their solutions. Reader response theory, the writing process, students' right to their own language, and other pedagogical concepts stressing the need to respect student endeavor have led many of us to confuse accepting students' ideas with respecting them, and this in turn has led to Perkins' hasty, narrow, fuzzy, and sprawling responses that we often receive. We need to be able to challenge students' responses, to make them think more deeply about a problem if they are to recognize when their responses will not result in appropriate solutions or when a better solution is possible. It is not only all right to say, "That answer is wrong"; it is required.

Mark Lehnerer has adapted the Socratic Seminar as a method for teaching students to ask appropriate questions as well as to question others' solutions. He uses the method in his world literature class. Basing his objectives on Adler's concepts (1983), he explains that the object of the seminar is to "stimulate the capacity of participants to think independently." The focus is on sharing ideas rather than on covering material, that is, quality over quantity. Mark has adopted this method, because he has found that it (1) serves as an excellent springboard for writing, (2) encourages all students to become involved, (3) moves students along all levels of Bloom's taxonomy, and (4) is "FUN!" He has also found that students like it because it allows them to express their opinions without fear of ridicule, it encourages them to take risks, and it is "FUN!"

Teaching a Socratic Seminar[*]

Marc Lehnerer, Munster High School

One of the most challenging aspects of using a Socratic Seminar is that as a teacher I have to learn to hold my tongue. In a traditional lecture/discussion format, the teacher asks questions and then waits for an answer. The students know, however, from years of personal experience that if they simply don't answer, the teacher will answer the question for them—typically in five to ten seconds. The Socratic Seminar method compels students to be active participants in the learning process—or else the process comes to a halt. Of course, I've had Seminar sessions where the discussion falls apart—and those are the times that I've had to remind my students that they are responsible for their own learning, and that if they fail to take something from the discussion, it's likely their own fault.

Once the students have gained a sense of ownership of the discussion, it's amazing to see what they are capable of doing. They begin to understand that their opinions, backed up with reasonable evidence, are the real basis of the discussion, and they work feverishly to convince others of their ideas. They dive into the texts and often bring in outside sources of information. Imagine—students doing research not because they are assigned to do it, but because it will further their own learning! That's what I call teaching your students to think: helping to empower them to take charge of their own learning. That's the benefit of the Socratic Seminar.

Socratic Seminars help teachers achieve curricular goals, in a way that also encourages students to become self reliant. Once I learned to be the "guide on the side" rather than the "sage on the stage" (something I heard in college but never really understood) I found that with the right bits of prodding, with probing questions and broad-based discussion topics, the students reached my goals and enjoyed the learning process at the same time.

During a Socratic Seminar on Shakespeare's *Othello,* I nearly jumped out of my seat when one of my students, without any coaching from me, pointed out that Desdemona is a static character who doesn't undergo any changes throughout the course of the play, that it is only Othello's perception of her that changes. The student was proud of herself because she came to her own

[*]For more information on conducting Socratic seminars, see *The Performance Assessment Handbook, Portfolios and Socratic Seminars,* Volume I, by Bil Johnson, Princeton, NJ: Eye on Education, Inc. 1996.

conclusion, which the class accepted and which was later used as a basis for further discussion; I was proud of her because she fulfilled one of my points in teaching the work without my having to provide the information.

The key to the Socratic Seminar is to hold students accountable. One of the few times that I find myself getting involved in the discussion is to ask students "Where did you get that from?" or "Could you quote that line to the class?" Without stating it directly, I'm advocating to my students that they learn to use evidence to support their facts; they must back up their opinions. It's a valuable lesson to learn and transfer to all of their other classes. If they can't back up their claims with facts, their opinion doesn't really mean anything, both to their fellow students and to me, their evaluator. The same could be said for opinions in the real world.

So, without stating it directly, the Socratic method of teaching helps students learn to think. It makes them accountable for their own learning, and it forces them to back up their assertions with evidence. I don't know whether they will be able to quote from Shakespeare ten years from now, but I believe they will have the ability to make a reasoned, informed argument.

Appropriate Attitude

During the past decade we have heard a great deal about helping students acquire a positive attitude toward school and learning. However, a positive attitude toward learning is not sufficient. Students must also recognize that to engage in tasks that require higher order critical thinking skills, they need to expend a good deal of effort and time working to find the best solution and they need to persist in their endeavors, overcoming failures, until they arrive at a solution. Furthermore they must be willing to assume responsibility for their own learning, recognizing that without persistence on their part they will not learn the knowledges they need to acquire nor will they receive credit for what they have not learned.

Students need to develop what Dewey calls "Habits of mind" (Kolodner, 2002) that includes a disposition to expend effort to learn (Halpern, 1998). "Learners need to understand and be prepared for the effortful nature of critical thinking so they do not abandon the process too soon, believing that the thinking should have been easier or accomplished more quickly. The development of expertise in any area requires deliberate, effortful, and intense cognitive work" (Wagner, 1997, cited in Halpern, 1998). According to Halpern engaging in critical thinking requires a "willingness to engage in and persist at a complex task, the suppression of impulsive activity, flexibility and open-mindedness, and a willingness to abandon nonproductive strategies in an attempt to self correct" (52). Weinstein (1996) believes that underlying students' willingness to expend the effort and time required for learning is the students' desire to learn. "Students must want to learn—effective learning requires the will to set and accomplish reasonable learning goals." Without motivation to learn, students will not be willing to expend the effort and time.

Tim had certainly learned that learning took time, effort, and persistence. At some point after high school, Tim must have become motivated to complete a college education and somewhere he had decided that he would do whatever was necessary to meet this goal. Thus, he had been willing to persist in taking the developmental writing course until he passed, though it took three times. But in the end he had passed, his persistence being rewarded at last. Thus, having received reinforcement for the time and effort he expended, he was willing to engage in learning again, believing that eventually he would succeed.

For Tim and most of our students, learning that involves higher order cognitive skills is not easy. Understanding a poem requires rereading it several times; writing an effective essay requires revising it several times. Both require time in solitude to reflect on the work in progress—two luxuries that most working-class students do not have as we learned in Chapter 1. Furthermore, these tasks require "self-regulation" (Weinstein, 1996). Students must be willing to take responsibility for their own learning. To paraphrase an old adage, "You can lead a horse to water, but you can't make him drink"; you can teach a student all of the strategies for learning to learn, but without the will to do so, the student will not expend the time and effort necessary. Students need to recognize that if they are not willing to expend this time and effort, they will not succeed at their tasks.

Many of our students do not understand this aspect of education. Once again the reason is partially related to their culture, partially to their previous educational experiences. Because the atmosphere prescribed by many educators has been one of nurturing during the past decade, students have often become used to being hand fed, given step-by-step assistance in completing projects and mastering skills. Although the methods used are based on sound pedagogical theory, they have often been bastardized in their adaptation. For example, peer review, instead of being the final step in the revision process, often becomes the first step. Many students simply submit their drafts for review without expending the time required to evaluate and then revise their own work first. Their first drafts are truly first drafts. Although theoretically peer response, based on procedures followed by professional writers, is supposed to encourage students to engage in revision, in reality it often eliminates the need for students to take responsibility for evaluating and revising their own work. Peer review remains an important strategy for achieving an effective written text, but safeguards need to be built into the process to ensure that students have engaged in their own reviews and revisions before submitting work to their peers or teachers for review.

Today's students often feel that they do not need to meet a deadline if they have a "legitimate" excuse. In an effort to provide for personal problems, etc., teachers often move deadlines back or accept a wide variety of excuses to allow students to turn in work late without penalty. Yet, if an activity is assigned that provides students with sufficient time to work on it, students should be able to meet a deadline regardless of the circumstances. They are usually only unable to meet it if they have procrastinated in working on it.

While both the assistance in writing and the lack of pressure have been instituted with the best intentions, they may in many ways have actually hindered students' learning because these methods eliminate the effort required to learn. When we talk about raising standards, we should not talk about raising required grade point averages, but rather about raising standards related to quality of work, and to such aspects as meeting deadlines.

Other methods that schools have adopted recently, such as grading students on their progress in a course rather than on some form of norm- or criterion-based assessment, gives students a false sense of accomplishment and decreases their recognition that a "disposition toward effortful work" is necessary. Many students fail to understand that effort is relative. The amount of effort that students put into a course is dependent on their ability to master the knowledge required. Some students need to exert a great deal of effort; others need to exert only a little. Students need to understand that in college they will receive a grade related to how well they have learned a content area, not to how much they have exerted themselves in learning it. In the end, the grade reflects only whether or not the content has been learned, not the amount of time spent learning it.

In addition, because many students come from working-class homes, they equate work in school with work on a job as we discussed in the first chapter. They assume that if they put in the necessary number of hours, they will get paid (receive a passing grade), and if they put in overtime (do extra credit), they will get extra pay (a higher grade). In college, you don't get points for effort, only results. And there is no extra credit. At the college level, students must either acquire the knowledges required in a course or fail the course; there is no credit for effort unless the effort results in the achievement of the goals.

Over the years Tim had recognized that time and effort were necessary ingredients to learning. He started working on assignments as soon as he got them, rather than the day before they were due, so that he had sufficient time to check decisions with me and then make changes before he turned in his paper for a grade. He made the effort to come to my office during office hours if he had a question, even though he didn't need to be on campus at that time. And he took the time to look over his paper because he was unsure of himself still, sometimes asking a peer to check it, other times going to the writing lab. Through all of this, he assumed the responsibility for his own learning as he made the decisions and drafted the papers before asking for help. In addition, neither I nor the lab provided him with the answers. Instead, we concentrated on his decision-making procedures. I required that he explain his reasoning for the decisions he made based on the criterion I had provided in my lectures, and the lab assistants required he check the grammar books for the rules he was questioning. Thus, he was able to gain confidence in his decision making as he discovered that his decisions were good ones. For Tim, the effort he put into the class paid off; he received an "A" because his documentation was well done.

Halpern (1998) recommends that we specifically tell students that "a thoughtful consideration of evidence and arguments will require the expenditure of mental effort," so that they do not expect quick and easy answers and will not be surprised by the amount of effort required of them.

Developing Instruction for Teaching Students to Learn to Learn

If we are to prepare high school students to succeed in college composition and literature courses, then we need to teach them to learn to learn, so that they can transfer the knowledges they acquire during the first twelve years in school to their new courses in higher education. Thus, it is imperative that we include procedural and conditional knowledge as well as declarative knowledge in our curriculum. Furthermore, in addition to teaching general strategies, such as note taking and annotating, that are relevant for learning in any content area regardless of whether it is English, chemistry, or welding, we need to provide instruction in domain-specific strategies, such as prereading and prewriting, that are related to specific content areas, such as literature and freshman composition. These strategies must be made overt through metacognition so that students can internalize them for backward-reaching transfer in their college courses.

Let's look at how instruction in domain-specific heuristics can be integrated into an English curriculum. Because it is easy to create workplace writing assignments that reflect real-world tasks and because many of the skills required in workplace writing are also required for academic writing, the following example involves a workplace writing unit that I often teach. The goal for the unit is that "Students will learn to write a proposal." In doing so, they will also learn to write persuasive discourse.

The prompt for the final assignment is as follows.

> You have noticed that something at school/home/work is a problem (ex., insufficient parking at school/the garbage disposal in your house that constantly gets clogged/not enough personnel to bag the groceries between 4 and 5:30 p.m. at the store where you work), and you think you know a way to solve it. You decide to write a memorandum to your teacher or principal/parents/supervisor proposing the solution. You will need to think about how you can persuade your reader to adopt your proposal.

Before the students can tackle the assignment, they need to engage in a series of lessons that helps them use their prior knowledge of other genres and discourses to learn the new genre—a proposal for change. Each lesson serves as a small step in a ladder, with each activity building on the previous one so that by the time the students are ready to learn the genre required by the prompt, they have amassed sufficient knowledge to do so easily. In using this approach, we can help students, as they participate in the various activities, acquire sufficient skills and strategies, that by the end of the unit they can write an effective persuasive paper. The lessons help students acquire the procedural knowledge they need to write an unfamiliar type of document by focusing on the heuristics they need to learn the conventions, text grammars, style (voice and tone), and visual aspects of a new genre.

The unit begins with a discussion of the kinds of correspondence students already know—thank you letters for presents and invitations to parties—thus making overt their prior knowledge. The discussion revolves around the conventions of social correspondence, such as the salutation and closing on the thank you letters, and the headings for name, address, time, date, and RSVP on invitations. It also provides an opportunity to discuss the text grammars; that is, letters require complete sentences; templates, such as those on invitations, simply require data. Furthermore, the discussion incorporates visual text, as the invitations include headings that are often in all capital letters. Because workplace writing often involves the graphic display of information and requires the formatting of a page, students need to become aware of the visual as well as the textual aspects of written communication. In addition, the discussions consider the *sounds* of thank you letters so that students can begin to consider voice, style, and tone. During this discussion, consideration is also given to the rhetorical aspects of audience, purpose, and situation and how these influence the content and style. Students also examine the persuasive elements in each letter. Thus, they begin acquiring a vocabulary with which to talk about workplace writing and persuasive discourse. To conclude the lesson, students work in small groups at the computer to create an invitation to a birthday party for a young relative in their family and to write a thank you letter to a relative who has just given them a pair of designer socks for their birthday. To be certain that they use the appropriate conventions, grammars, and visual text, they are required to refer to their notes as they write.

These papers are not graded; I simply move around the groups, checking that the appropriate conventions, text grammars, and visual text are being used. Often with the use of Power Point and clip art the documents are quite creative. The lesson concludes with the students engaging in metacognition so that they can internalize the processes in which they have been engaged. By asking them to think back on the steps they followed to write the letter and invitation, they become aware they engaged in the following processes:

- Thought about similar letters and invitations they had written or received and considered their respective conventions, text grammars, visual text, voice, style, and tone. They then used the letters and invitations with which they were familiar as models for writing the new letters.
- Considered how the audience, purpose, and context had influenced the voice, style, and tone of their previous letters.
- Considered how each letter included persuasive elements.

- Took or made notes of all relevant information in order to have a checklist in the future.
- Referred to notes to check that all aspects were included and were written correctly.

Students are then engaged in forward-reaching transfer as they are asked to think about ways they might use the strategies they have just learned to solve future problems. Eventually they recognize that they can use previously written documents as models for determining such aspects as conventions, text grammars, visual text, voice, style, and tone for a new similar document.

From the familiar social letter we move to the less familiar business letter, from a letter of invitation to a letter announcing a meeting for parents at a PTA. This lesson begins with backward-reaching transfer. Students are asked to think about what they learned in the previous lesson that they can use to learn to write a business letter. They have no difficulty recognizing that they can use letters they've seen previously as models and they can rattle off the aspects they need to consider, such as a heading, salutation, closing, and signature. Most students have seen business letters; they've received letters related to drivers' licenses and car accidents, and colleges and credit card companies have sent them letters soliciting their business. Again the discussion centers on what these letters *look* and *sound* like, and students' responses are recorded on the chalk board while they take notes. This time students begin to use the appropriate terms to describe the various aspects under consideration. After the discussion, copies of several business letters are disseminated, and students are asked to check the various aspects they find in these letters against the list they have generated. Additional items that they now find are added to the list on the chalk board. The entire class participates in writing the letter to the PTA. It is recorded on an overhead transparency so the students can see what is being written. The lesson ends as the previous one did by engaging students in metacognition. They are asked to think about what they did and then, engaging in forward-reaching transfer, they are asked to consider how they might use these heuristics in the future. The list they generate includes not only the heuristics from the previous lesson but also a new procedure: study actual examples of the document you are going to write.

The next lesson is concerned with another unfamiliar genre, the memorandum of request. This activity requires that they write to someone, such as the principal, requesting something, such as a file cabinet or bookcase or computer modem for their classroom. As the lesson begins, students are once again required to engage in backward-reaching transfer. As they consider whether or not they can use their previous experience to help them learn to write this new type of correspondence, they recognize that their prior experience is not sufficiently analogous to the present task to help them learn the conventions, etc. However, they recognize that they can learn the conventions for this new genre by examining a model of an actual memorandum. Once students arrive at this conclusion, they are provided with copies of several memoranda to examine, providing them with the opportunity to learn the conventions, voice, style, organization of information, and the kinds of content used in making a request. Next we talk about writing to persuade an audience in general and then relate the concepts to the specific mini-assignment. The class is then divided into small groups with each group writing a memorandum requesting something for the classroom. A member of each group reads the group's work to the entire class. Once again at the conclusion of the lesson, the students engage in metacognition to determine what they have learned and in forward-reaching transfer to consider how they can use what they have learned in the future.

Having identified and listed the basic aspects for this subgenre of correspondence and practiced writing it first in a large group with the teacher, then in a small group without the teacher, they are ready to draft their own personal memo, requesting something from a teacher, administrator, or supervisor. During the introduction to the assignment, they are once again engaged in backward-reaching transfer, considering what they have learned previously that they can use to engage in this assignment successfully. In most cases, students simply rely on their memories, but at least several students turn to their notes, thereby adding another procedure to their repertoire of learning to learn. They are now ready to engage in the writing process—planning, drafting, and revising their memos. It is expected that they know the process and will engage in it. These papers are graded.

Students are finally ready to move to the final assignment and to take responsibility for their own learning. Because students are unfamiliar with the context in which a proposal for change is used, the lesson is introduced with a lecture related to how this document is used in the workplace and the criteria that are used to judge it as acceptable or unacceptable. Once students have this information, they engage in backward-reaching transfer to determine how they can go about writing this unfamiliar document. By now many of them have begun to catch on. They recognize they can use models. These are then provided. But this time there is no class or small group discussion concerning the conventions, text grammar, visual text and graphics, layout, organizational structure, content, and style. Studying the examples to determine these aspects is now the students' responsibility. They are on their own. It is up to them to transfer the procedural knowledge they have gained in working on the previous writing assignments to this one.

Using metacognition to engage in backward- and forward-reaching transfer, students have learned the heuristics for determining how to write a workplace genre, and they have had a sufficient number of diverse assignments to develop the cognitive flexibility required to determine those aspects in previous models that can be transferred to writing in a new subgenre. At this point, they, not the teacher, need to expend energy and time working on the assignment. Grades for this assignment usually fall into three categories: (1) "A"/ high "B," indicating those students who have spent the time and effort to learn the features and conventions of the new genre and then engaged recursively in all phases of the writing process in order to write a good document; (2) "C," indicating those students who expended some effort to learn some of the features and conventions of the new genre and then drafted their document without spending much time in either the planning or revising phases; and (3) "F," indicating those students who did not expend the effort either to learn the features or conventions of the new genre or to engage in more than the drafting phase of the writing process.

Responsibilities: Ours and Theirs

In creating independent learners, we must be willing to stand back and allow our students to try to use their new knowledges. If we have constructed the scaffolding (our lessons) with sufficient care, then most of our students should be able to succeed on their own.

Several weeks ago I sat squinting in front of a microfiche machine, trying to make out the illegible words of a ninety-page report on "power writing," the latest fad to hit public education. It was eight o'clock on one of those beautiful cool evenings in June when I like to go for a stroll around the neighborhood, admiring the flocks of daisies a week of summer rain has raised in everyone's gardens. But the dimly lit, windowless library room let in none of that fading sunlight that colors the Midwest sky. Why am I doing this, I wondered. Then, suddenly, I realized I didn't have to. The teachers attending the National Writing Project workshop that I was conducting had asked about research related to "power writing" and I was trying to locate the information on it. Here I was doing exactly what I had been telling the teachers not to do with their students. I was doing their research for them. They needed to take responsibility for finding the answers to their own questions. I turned off the machine and exited into the cool night.

The next day I marched into the workshop with the bibliography I had collected from ERIC and the group split up into research teams. Three days later they had gathered more information than I could possibly have collected on my own in so short a time. Going beyond the bibliography, they had searched the Internet, gotten into some relevant chat rooms, collected workbooks and curriculum guides related to the topic, interviewed administrators who had brought the program into their schools, and e-mailed the founders of the program. By the time everyone reported their findings, the class had become experts on the topic of power writing. Three months later two of the members chaired a session on "power writing" at the annual meeting of the National Writing Project.

Just as we teachers must assume responsibility for determining the validity of the educational fads that periodically come into existence, our students must assume responsibility for learning our courses. We are responsible for learning and using effective methods in our classrooms, but in the end, they are responsible for their own learning.

If students are to be prepared for college classes, then they must be willing to expend the necessary effort to learn. They must also have acquired the procedural skills necessary for transferring information and using higher order thinking skills. Because academic literacy involves these skills, we need to teach students procedural as well as declarative knowledge. The remainder of this book is concerned with the various kinds of domain-specific procedural knowledge that students need to know if they are to succeed in college composition and literature courses.

References

Adey, Philip, and Micheal Shayer. 1993. "An Exploration of Long-Term Far-Transfer Effects Following an Extended Intervention Program in the High School Science Curriculum." *Cognition and Instruction*. 11.1: 1–29.

Adey, Philip, and Michael Shayer. *Really Raising Standards*. London: Routledge.

Adler, Mortimer. 1983. *Paideia Problems and Possibilities*. New York: McMillan Publishing Company.

Bassok, Miriam. 1990. "Transfer of Domain-Specific Problem-Solving Procedures." *Journal of Experimental Psychology: Learning, Memory and Cognition*. 16: 522–33.

Bloom, Benjamin. 1956. *Taxonomy of Educational Objectives*. New York: David McKay Company, Inc.

Bridges, Edwin M. 1992. *Problem-Based Learning for Administrators*. Eugene, OR: The Educational Resources Information Center Clearinghouse on Educational Management.

Brown, Ann. 1987. "Metacognition, Executive Control, Self-Regulation, and Other More Mysterious Mechanisms." In *Metacognition, Motivation, and Understanding,* edited by Franz E. Weinert and Rainer H. Kluwe. Hillsdale, NJ: Erlbaum.

Brown, Richard H. 1996. "Learning How to Learn: The Amherst Project and History Education in the Schools." *The Social Studies*. 267–73.

Bruer, John T. 1993. *Schools for Thought: A Science of Learning in the Classroom*. Cambridge, MA: MIT Press.

Bruner, Jerome. 1979. "Learning How To Do Things with Words. In *Psycholinguistic Research,* edited by D. Aaronson and R.W. Reiber, 265–84. Hillsdale, NJ: Erlbaum.

Caine, Renate Nummela, and Geoffrey Caine. 1991. *Making Connections: Teaching and the Human Brain*. Arlington, VA: Association for Supervision and Curriculum Development.

Cervone, Daniel. 1993. "The Role of Self-Referent Cognitions in Goal Setting, Motivation, and Performance." In *Cognitive Science Foundations of Instruction*, edited by Mitchell Rabinowitz, 57–95. Hillsdale, NJ: Erlbaum.

Delisle, Robert. 1997. *How To Use Problem-Based Learning in the Classroom*. Arlington, VA: Association of Supervision and Curriculum Development.

Erwin, Robin W. 1985. "Research Currents for Developmental Reading Educators: Metacognition." *Research and Teaching in Developmental Education* 2(1): 19–23.

Feathers, Karen M., and Jane H. White. 1987. "Learning to Learn: Case Studies of the Process." *Reading Research and Instruction* 26: 264–74.

Flower, Linda. 1985. *Problem-Solving Strategies for Writing*. San Diego: Harcourt, Brace Jovanovich, Publishers.

Garafalo, Joe. 1986. "Metacognitive Knowledge and Metacognitive Process: Important Influences on Mathematical Performance." *Research and Teaching Developmental Education* 2(2): 34–39.

Gentner, Dedre, and Keith J. Holyoak. 1997. "Reasoning and Learning by Analogy: Induction." *American Psychologist* 52(1): 32–4.

Gentner, Dedre, and Arthur B. Markman. 1997. "Structure Mapping in Analogy and Similarity" *American Psychologist*. 52(1): 45–56.

Halpern, Diane F. 1998. "Teaching Critical Thinking for Transfer Across Domains: Dispositions, Skills, Structure Training, and Metacognitive Monitoring." *American Psychologist*. 4: 449–55.

Hammond, Kristian J., et al. 1991. "Functionality in Analogical Transfer: A Hard Match Is Good To Find." *The Journal of the Learning Sciences*. 1: 111–52.

Hunter, Madeline. 1971. *Teach for Transfer*. El Segundo, CA: TIP Publications.

Keane, Mark. 1987. "On Retrieving Analogues When Solving Problems." *The Quarterly Journal of Experimental Psychology* 39: 29–41.

Kochevar, L. K., and Paul E. Johnson. 1988. "Problem Solving Is What You Do When You Don't Know What To Do." *Proceedings of the Tenth Annual Conference of the Cognitive Science Society*. Hillsdale, NJ: Erlbaum. Associates, Publisher. 615–23

Kolodner, Janet L. 1997. "Educational Implications of Analogy: A View from Case-Based Reasoning." *American Psychologist* 52(1): 57–66.

Kolodner, Janet L. 2002. Unpublished manuscript.

Kolodner, Janet L., et al. 1998. "Learning by Design from Theory to Practice." *Proceedings of the Third International Conference on the Learning Sciences*. Charlottesville, VA: AACE.

Langer, Judith A. 1999. *Beating the Odds: Teaching Middle and High School Students To Read and Write Well*. Report Series 12014. Albany, NY: National Research Center on English Learning and Achievement.

Marzano, Robert J. 1991. *Cultivating Thinking in English*. Urbana, IL: National Council of Teachers of English.

Marzano, Robert J., Ronald Brandt, et al. 1988. *Dimensions of Thinking: A Framework for Curriculum and Instruction*. Arlington, VA: Association of Supervision and Curriculum Development.

Miller, George A. 1956. "The Magical Number Seven Plus or Minus Two: Sum Limits to Our Capacity for Processing Information. *Psychological Review* 6(3): 81–97.

Novick, Laura. 1988. "Analogical Transfer, Problem Similarity, and Expertise." *Journal of Experimental Psychology*. 14(3): 510–20.

Perkins, David N., and Tina A. Grotzer. 1997. "Teaching Intelligence." *American Psychologist* 52(10): 1125–33.

Pressley, Michael, Barbara L. Snyder, and Teresa Cariglia-Bull. 1987. "How Can Good Strategy Use Be Taught to Children? Evaluation of Six Alternative Approaches." In *Transfer of Learning: Contemporary Research and Applications*. Edited by Stephen M. Cormier and Joseph D. Hagman. San Diego: Academic Press.

Ross, Brian H. 1989. "Distinguishing Types of Superficial Similarities: Different Effects on the Access and Use of Earlier Problems." *Journal of Experimental Psychology: Learning, Memory and Cognition*.15(3): 456–68.

Salomon, Gabriel, and David N. Perkins. 1989. "Rocky Roads to Transfer: Rethinking Mechanisms of a Neglected Phenomenon." *Educational Psychologist* 24(2): 113–42.

Schoenfeld, Alan H. 1979. "Explicit Heuristic Training as a Variable in Problem-Solving Performance." *Journal of Research in Mathematics Education* 10: 173–87.

Singley, Mark K., and John R. Anderson. 1989. *The Transfer of Cognitive Skill*. Cambridge, MA: Harvard University Press

Spiro, Rand J., et al. 1988. "Cognitive Flexibility Theory: Advanced Knowledge Acquisition in Ill-Structured Domains." *Proceedings of the Tenth Annual Conference of the Cognitive Science Society,* 375–88. Hillsdale, NJ: Erlbaum.

Sternberg, Robert J., and Peter A. Frensch. 1993. "Mechanisms of Transfer." In *Transfer on Trial: Intelligence, Cognition, and Instruction*, 25–38. Norwood, NJ: Ablex Publishing Corporation.

Weinstein, Claire, Ellen. 1996. "Learning How to Learn: An Essential Skill for the 21st Century." *Educational Record* 49–52.

Weinstein, Claire E., and Debra K. Meyer. 1991. "Cognitive Learning Strategies and College Teaching." *New Directions for Teaching and Learning* 45: 15–26.

3

Domain-Specific Heuristics for Composition

Helping Students Write Academic Prose

Carolyn Boiarsky

I am convinced more and more, day by day, that fine writing is next to fine doing, the top thing in the world.
   —John Keats in a letter to J. H. Reynolds, 24 August, 1819

A person who sees Quality and feels it as he works is a person who cares.
   —Robert Persig, The Art of Motorcycle Maintenance, 1976

To learn to write, students need an environment that is both challenging and comfortable. They need to be challenged to think more deeply and to express their thoughts more effectively. But they also need to feel comfortable trying out new ideas and new ways of expressing themselves. We need to consider carefully which scaffolds should be removed and when, and which should remain. And we need to recognize that we may have to build additional scaffolding as we introduce students to new strategies. Such scaffolding must take students from where they are to the level required in the academy.

By the time students reach their senior year at Purdue University Calumet, all scaffolding has been removed and they are left standing on their own, required to demonstrate that they can do so by completing a senior project. In the professional writing program, they are given a real-world assignment in which they are expected to produce a document that will actually be used by someone in the industry or at the university. One of the most successful projects that students have completed is a catalog of teacher workshops for the Northwest Indiana Writing Project. The catalog, which involves over 100 entries, was a joint project undertaken by two nontraditional students.

Melodie and Linda represent the new breed of women students who are returning to college. Although both are in their early thirties, they look closer to eighteen. Raised in working-class families, they married and had children immediately after high school. But the marriages didn't last and they discovered they needed to have their own careers, so they returned to the local college. They have since remarried, but they are continuing to work toward a degree. Maintaining a high B average, Melodie has been attending college while working as a full-time receptionist at a local car dealership and raising two children, the oldest of whom is 13. Linda, who will graduate with honors, had her second child during the last week of the spring semester and returned the following week to take her finals.

Although both students had taken courses in technical writing, desktop publishing, and software documentation, neither had learned to create a catalog. But the result was a "quality" publication that was put together so well it could have served as a coffee table decoration (see Figure 3–1).

When they brought their first draft to me I was thrilled.

"I remembered you told us that if we saw something we liked, we should adapt it," Melodie explained. "I found this catalog at the car dealership where I work and we liked it so much we decided to copy it."

"We used everything we learned from you and Professor Dobberstein and Professor Mabrito," Linda continued. "Every time we started to do something, we'd remember something one of you said."

I don't think there is any greater reward a writing teacher can have than this.

Melodie and Linda had used the strategies that they learned in their various classes about information design to create a quality product. Perceiving writing as a problem-solving activity, they had gone about their assignment by applying to their new project a set of previously learned domain-specific heuristics. It is this set of heuristics that students need to acquire if they are to succeed in writing in the academy and in the workplace beyond.

Although the heuristics discussed in this chapter do not encompass all of the strategies that writers use, they are the main ones, and they provide students with much of the information they need for making appropriate decisions related to the problems inherent in any written assignment. The first two strategies—reading like a writer and analyzing the audience—help writers develop the frame—content, organization, style, and format—for their texts. The ones that follow—dialoging with authors, chunking related information, learning by trial and error, collaborating, developing voices, integrating the expressive with the transactional—provide strategies for creating effective and even elegant texts. Little space is devoted to the final strategy—engaging in the process—as so much has already been written about it. By helping students acquire this process knowledge, we can help them succeed in the various writing assignments they are required to do in college.

Figure 3–1 Northwest Indiana Writing Project Catalog Cover

Reading Like a Writer

Melodie discovered how to organize the information about the workshops of the Writing Project and how to lay out the catalog by "reading like a writer" (Smith, 1984). She didn't read the commercial catalog to learn about the products in it, but rather to *see* how it was put together. To read like a writer means to read to discover *how* a writer has written a text rather than to read for content, to discover *what* a writer is writing about. Because during their academic career students need to write in a variety of genres for a wide range of fields, they need to be able to read like a writer so that they can write in new genres and new fields.

If students are to learn to write in a specific genre or subgenre, then they need to read documents in that genre. They cannot write in a genre that they have never read. If they are expected to use metaphorical language effectively, then they need to read texts that use this rhetorical device. By examining how authors manipulate texts, students not only become aware of the choices writers make, but they begin to learn to consciously make these choices themselves. "When writers read, they see the text behind the text, what was not said, the choices the writer made, the problems solved and not solved (Murray, 1993, p. 2).

By reading like a writer, students can also learn how a literary analysis differs from a biology lab report, and they can begin to understand why they cannot apply the same "rules" or conventions to a lab report that they apply to an analysis. If they are to write successfully, they need to recognize that whereas in a paper for an English class paragraphs are long, in an engineering class they are short. In an essay for English composition, items in a list are placed in paragraph form and connected with transitions, such as "first," "second," "next," "then"; in a biology report items are listed and connected by sequencing them numerically. In a literary analysis references are cited using the MLA style, in the sciences a numerical system is used, and in technology the author/date system is used. History uses a different citation system altogether.

If students are to learn to write academic genres and subgenres, then they need to find papers written in the various subject areas and study the conventions used in each of the respective fields. As they read the documents, they should examine the following ten features.

1. Introduction/conclusion—how does the writer introduce/conclude the document?

2. Content—what information is included and what is eliminated?

3. Organization—what organizational structure does the author use? How does the author sequence information?

4. Style—on what reading level does the writer write? Are sentences, paragraphs short or long? Are many words multisyllabic or of Greek and Latin roots, or mainly short, Anglo Saxon in origin? Are technical words used?

5. Conventions—what conventions do you notice? (e.g., Does the paper include an abstract? Does the letter include a subject line in the heading?)

6. Text grammars—what are the grammatical rules for this document? (e.g., Instructions are written in active voice, imperative mood; abstracts for engineering documents are often written in passive voice.)

7. Visualization—are there headings, subheadings? Are there lists using bullets or numbers? Are there spaces between the items in a list? Are there boxes for special information? Is the title centered? Are the headings in all capital letters? Are they bold faced?

8. Graphics—are there charts, tables, pictures, cartoons?

9. Argument—what is considered an appropriate argument in the field, and what is considered a valid point?

10. Citations—how are sources cited and referenced in the field?

When I teach introductory technical writing classes, I introduce each assignment by helping students learn how these features appear in the type of document they will be writing. Because many students have never read a proposal or a letter of request or a final report, they have no idea what these documents look or sound like or how information is presented in them. I ask students to examine three examples of the same kind of document, such as a memorandum, and determine the similarities and differences among the three in relation to the ten features. Students can engage in a similar activity in literature classes when they are assigned to write literary analyses. Instead of examining proposals, they can study articles from the MLA and other literary journals. By studying several examples of specific genres or subgenres, students become aware of the conventions that are used and begin to replicate them in their own documents. If they conclude that the authors of proposals use a problem/solution organizational structure, then they do so in writing their own proposals for a science or engineering course. If they recognize that in literary analyses the authors use quotes from texts to support their points, then they do so in their analyses also.

A colleague who teaches review writing introduces students to the genre by handing out reviews from the *New Yorker*, the *Chicago Tribune*, the local Hammond, Indiana, newspaper, and the student newspaper and asks his students to read the reviews like writers. He not only wants them to discover what a review entails—the content, focus, organization, and style—but he wants them to learn how the focus and style differ, depending on the readers.

To help students in their comparisons, I provide a handout that is divided into four columns. Students list the ten features in the first column. In the other columns they describe how the various features are handled in each of the three respective examples. After they have completed the chart, I ask them to come up with a generalization related to how a particular type of document handles each feature. Only after they have worked through the worksheet for these texts do they write their own documents.

Hagemann (1999) believes that teaching students to read like writers helps them see that authors "have control over their texts and that good writing comes from making sound choices." She believes that "It's especially important that basic writing students see writing as a series of choices or problems to be solved, because many of them believe that writing is a talent that you either get or you don't. . . Because they see writing as a talent, they don't believe they can learn to be better writers. But if they begin to see writing as choices they make, then they're motivated to learn."

In teaching her students to read like writers, Hagemann (1999) takes them through a five-step process developed by Ray (1999). The process involves students (1) noticing a feature, (2) theorizing why the author chose the feature, (3) naming the technique the author uses, (4) comparing the text to other texts that have used the technique, and (5) envisioning (a form of forward-reaching transfer) using the technique in their own writing.

In one class, Hagemann wanted her students to learn to write introductions to catch a reader's attention. She engaged them in the following steps.

1. *Noticing.* Students examine several previously written papers that exemplify a variety of attention-grabbing introductions, including a personal anecdote, a shocking statistic, and a dramatic quote.

2. *Theorizing.* Students discuss why these introductions are effective, whether one is more effective than another, and the relationship between the attention grabber and the thesis of the piece.

3. *Naming.* Students develop a vocabulary that allows them to talk about style and style elements, such as parallel structure, text grammars, metaphors, anecdotes, and dialog. In this case students use the term "attention grabber" to explain that part of the introduction that is aimed at getting the reader's attention.

4. *Comparing.* Students are given examples of introductions that do and do not "work" and discuss the reasons a personal anecdote works in one paper but not in another.

5. *Envisioning.* Students think about how they might use an "attention grabber" in their next paper.

The result of this exercise is that instead of the typical introductions to so many first-year compositions, for example, "In today's society," "Many people believe. . .," students in this class wrote introductions that made the reader, even the instructor, want to read further.

Writing for an Audience

During the past quarter of a century, there has been a great deal of emphasis on assigning students to write for audiences other than for the teacher (Britton et al., 1975; Ede and Lunsford, 1984). However, in the academy, the teacher is actually the audience for whom students must write, and students know this. Even when students are provided with scenarios, they continue to try to "psyche out" the teacher. "What does she want?" is the hue and cry. Ashley (2001) found that proficient working-class students talked a great deal about "giving teachers what they want" in terms of writing academic papers (505). Some, she found, perceived this as "playing the school game" and "writing what will be accepted" (504–5). In fact, that is exactly what the "writing game" is all about.

These students are doing exactly what we tell them to do—analyze your readers and then write for them. They know that in the academy the audience is the teacher and the purpose is for a grade. This situation occurs especially in content courses, including those in literature. But this "game" is not limited to the academy. Writers who wish to publish must write on topics they know are of current interest to editors, and they must write in a style that reflects the audience for that particular publication. The editor for *Time Magazine* will not publish an article written in the style of the *MLA Journal* or vice versa. This game is also played in the workplace where employees write for their supervisors and clients. A busy executive does not want to read through long paragraphs written in narrative style to discover the recommendations from a feasibility report that she commissioned, and a biologist reading a scientific journal wants to be able to check the procedures used in a study, not just read the results as she would in a magazine for the general public.

Just as writers need to be able to write for different audiences and different purposes, to succeed in college students need to learn to write for different professors in different fields. Thus, in literature classes, students should have opportunities to write analyses for their teachers so that they can begin to learn how to write in that field, just as they need to write papers for the teachers of their history and chemistry classes.

Analyzing an audience involves three phases: (1) analyzing the reader, (2) interpreting the analysis, and (3) applying the interpretation to a specific writing assignment. In the first phase writers must determine the answers to the following questions.

1. What do my readers know in terms of content about my topic and what don't they know?

2. What do my readers want to know about the topic?

3. What are my readers biases toward my topic?

4. Will my readers understand technical terminology related to the topic?

The second and third questions are of prime importance in the academy. In some instances, teachers know the content and simply want to know if students know it also. However, at other times, teachers may not know very much about a topic but may want to learn about it or learn their students' perceptions of the topic. The latter is often the case in freshman composition. In literature classes, teachers may be as interested in how students interpret a text as they are in what students know about the text. As for biases, the latter teachers may be biased toward a gender interpretation or a political interpretation.

Once students have analyzed their readers, they must learn to interpret the results of their analysis. This interpretation serves as the basis for their responses to the following set of questions.

- What content should I include and what should I exclude?
- What arguments should I use to overcome my audience's negative biases and to build on my audience's positive biases?
- What style should I use?

If students are writing for a teacher who wants to know what they know, then students need to include as much information from the teacher's lectures and textbook assignments as possible. However, if they are writing for a teacher who is interested in learning how gender theory can be applied to Keats' poetry, then they need to limit their information to this topic.

By asking students to write for a variety of academic purposes and fields, we can help them learn to write for different audiences. In the real world, including the academic world, the audience is a given, that is, a supervisor, a client, or a biologist. Writers do not select their readers, but rather they write to a particular audience. They may need to submit reports to those in charge of their projects, request something from their supervisors, or respond to requests from their clients.

If we are going to truly teach students to write for different audiences and for different purposes, then we need to provide them with real "others" to whom to write. If we are going to help them learn to write for various academic readers, then we need to provide assignments that require they write for teachers in a variety of fields. Thus, integrating English with other content areas, such as science or technology, provides students with opportunities to write for "others," that is, their biology, chemistry, or technology teacher. [For other discussions on integrating English with science and technology, see Boiarsky (1997).]

Dialoging with Authors

Many students have difficulty using the background readings they are assigned as springboards for considering and reconsidering ideas that they can present in a paper. In many cases they do not take the time to discover relationships between the author's ideas and their own thoughts and experiences. They hurry through a text, attempting to understand what the writer is saying but not attempting to integrate the writer's ideas with their own.

Many professional writers are slow readers. One of the reasons is that they want to absorb the text, to read each word until they know that author's style and thoughts so well that they can almost reproduce them. Another reason is that they find themselves caught up in the writer's thoughts. They may agree with the writer's ideas and want to add some of their own knowledge to the author's text, or they may be diametrically opposed to the ideas and want to argue with them. A description may recall a similar place or feeling in their own lives, a dialog may evoke one they would like to have. As these thoughts surface, they stop reading and indulge their fantasies. They hold a dialog with the author, arguing with the ideas being presented or supporting the ideas with their own. It is these silent discussions that provide the basis for essays, feature articles, and literary analyses.

Students often think that they should be able to read quickly. Many perceive being a "slow reader" as tantamount to being a "slow learner." Pausing in their reading to think about something the author has just written is often perceived as day-dreaming, something they have been told not to do. Students need to recognize that taking time from their reading to think about some aspect of what they have just read can provide the kind of deep thinking that we want to find in student papers. We need to let students know that they have our permission to engage in this day-dreaming activity and that, in fact, we encourage it.

In addition to overtly telling students that we spend time away from our reading to dialog with authors, we should create situations in which students are required to engage in this kind of thinking. By providing topics around which students must structure their journals and annotations, we can influence students to pause at various points in their reading. If students are expected to annotate the changes in Jane Eyre's perceptions of Rochester, then they not only notice these changes as they are presented in the text but also begin to think about them. (Burdan in Chapter 6 discusses the importance of annotating.) Thus, when students are asked to write a paper concerning Jane Eyre as a modern woman, they have already thought a good deal about her.

Chunking Related Information

One of the greatest difficulties students have in writing academic papers is in organizing the information they've collected. They need to become aware of the many patterns in which they can organize data and to learn to determine which of these patterns is appropriate for the content and field in which they are writing. By teaching them to read like a writer, we can help them discover the overall patterns of various genres. By analyzing the genre in which they have been assigned to write, they can discover the major sections into which their information should be organized. For example, they can discover that a literary analysis begins with an introduction, establishing the writer's topic, and then goes on to briefly describe the work before discussing the major points of the analysis in great detail. A conclusion sums up the writer's stance.

But this strategy only provides a structure for the major parts of a paper; it does not provide help for organizing the information that goes into each part. The writer is left to decide how this information should be sequenced. This decision is further complicated when some of the information appears to be relevant to more than one of the points. There are no rules or conventions, no easy solutions, to this problem. However, a technique using chunking, developed by Van Nostrand, Knoblauch, and Pettigrew (1982), can be especially helpful in planning an organized academic paper (Boiarsky, 1986). Using this method, writers organize data into larger and larger chunks of information by following a seven-step process.

1. List all of the data collected.

2. Examine the data to determine which pieces of information are related to each other. The easiest way to do this is to use symbols to indicate the different relationships; that is, an asterisk indicates information related to characterization; a plus sign indicates information related to the use of dialog, a square indicates information related to description of one character by another, etc.

3. Put related information together in categories and give each category a name that summarizes the information in it. You may have several pieces of information in more than one category.

4. Determine in which category information that has been placed in more than one category should go.

5. Write a sentence that serves as an organizing idea for each category. Use the category name in the sentence.

6. Sequence the categories.

7. Write the paper following the sequence of the categories and using the organizing idea for each category as the topic sentence for that section of your paper.

Despite the amount of work a writer puts into the prewriting phase to organize data, and the amount of internal revision (Murray, 1968) in which the writer engages during drafting, the final result of a first draft can often be described as repetitive and chaotic. This is because writing is discovery; through our writing we discover what we are going to say (Vygotsky, 1962). In this situation, revision becomes imperative and chunking can be a helpful technique for determining how to revise the information. This time, as writers read their drafts, they indicate in the margin next to each paragraph (chunk) the category to which it belongs. During this process, writers often find that a chunk of information (sentence or paragraph) on page 2 is related to data on page 6. The writer can then "cut and paste" the related pieces of information together and place them on either page 6 or page 2.

Another technique for helping students discover related chunks of information that are scattered throughout a text or to discover redundant information is to assign them to make an oral presentation using Power Point. As students create an outline from their papers that can serve as the main points in their presentation, they often discover that they have duplicated data or separated information that belongs in the same category.

It is a messy business, but no one has yet come up with a better way to write effectively.

Learning by Trial and Error

Students need to learn how to use the suggestions they receive during peer response sessions and from instructors to improve not just the text on which they are working but future texts.

During the past quarter of a century much has been written about helping students "correct" errors and improve their writing (Hull, 1985). Suggestions have included placing no more than three comments on a paper because students cannot deal with more, giving positive feedback prior to negative remarks, and providing macro, content-related help. Shaughnessy (1977) stresses the need to look beyond individual errors and to diagnose students' overall problems. It was hoped that by engaging in the writing process, which provides time for revision and proofreading, students would learn to improve their texts as they worked through multiple drafts. In many cases this did not happen.

The causes are multiple, but one of the major reasons is that many students do not seem to learn from previous successes or failures. They appear to perceive each new writing assignment either as the same as the previous one or as completely different, thereby applying either the same conventions when genres are different or different conventions when the genres are similar. Many of the students in my business writing course tend to sign a memorandum as they would a letter instead of simply initialing the memo, which is the appropriate convention.

We can help students learn to use their previous experiences in writing to engage successfully in a new writing assignment by helping them learn from their failures. While the strategies suggested over the past twenty-five years continue to be valid—bleeding all over a student's paper with red ink is both inappropriate and useless—we need to begin removing some of the scaffolding that we constructed when they entered elementary school. We need to allow them to make mistakes, to fail, and to try again.

Learning from Failure

In an effort to persuade students to think about how the suggestions I make on their papers can help them improve their texts, I engage them in an activity, using forward- and backward-reaching transfer. When I return their first paper, I ask them to set up a chart with five columns in which the first two are fairly wide and the final three are just wide enough for a check mark. In the first column, they list all of the problems indicated on their paper, such as the following: (1) Introduction does not relate to the paper; (2) paragraph 3 doesn't follow logically from paragraph 2; (3) two words are spelled wrong. In the next column I ask them to indicate how they might correct the errors and solve the problems. Then, before they submit their next paper, I have them use the list to check that they have not repeated any of the errors in their new assignment. When they get their second paper back, they place a check in the third column next to any of these items that are incorrect again. In addition, they add any new items to the list.

To make this approach even more effective, students should be required to correct their errors and solve their problems by revising each paper prior to writing the next one and then entering what they have done in the second column. The difficulty with this form of extended revision is that the paper should be reviewed by the instructor again to determine whether or not the revisions are appropriate. If we were able to teach to "mastery," then this process should continue until the students have revised their papers successfully. However, limitations in time—the system's, the student's, and the instructor's—often make this impossible to carry out.

Assuming Responsibility for Discourse Decisions

Cognitive psychologists again and again stress the need for students to be willing to make the effort and to spend the time necessary to learn. Students need to understand that writing is not easy, that revision takes time, and that creating a document that demonstrates deep thinking and logical sequencing takes a great deal of effort.

All too often, students ask us questions that, if they take the time to think about them, they can answer themselves. In some cases, they are unsure of their abilities and look for support for their decisions; in other cases, they have not bothered to spend the time required to solve their problems. We need to wean them from relying on our knowledge and require them to make some decisions on their own. For example, students in writing a comparison/contrast are often unsure whether to use an aabb or an abab organizational pattern and ask me which to use. I respond by admitting that there is no rule for determining the correct pattern. The only way to determine which is best is to try both, and I send them off to do so. Some make the effort to create a draft for each pattern and then select the one they believe is best. Some plan to draft both patterns but find their first attempt satisfactory and stop at that point, while others select a pattern at random and use it, regardless of whether or not it works because they do not want to expend the effort to try a second pattern. These latter students need to know not only if their pattern doesn't work but they also the consequences (a low grade) for failing to expend the effort to write one that does work.

I often respond to students' questions with ones of my own, forcing them to think through their questions in order to come up with the answers themselves.

In the technical writing class, when students ask me whether or not they should use a technical term, I reply, "What are the criteria for determining that?" They have no difficulty responding that it depends on the audience, as that is a key point that I repeat on a daily basis. "Well," I pick up the conversation, "will your audience understand the technical term you're thinking of using?" Again they have no difficulty responding yes or no. However, sometimes they're not sure. "Well, which would be the best way to go?" I ask. Once again, their common sense comes through. "To make sure they understand," they reply. "You've just answered your own question," I tell them.

Not only do students often ask us to do their leg work, but they also ask us to assume the responsibility for revising their work. Often the manuscripts that students use for peer response or hand in to the teacher are simply their first try. In such instances, the students are asking us to put the time and effort into their papers that they should have put into them. "What is written without effort is in general read without pleasure" (Samuel Johnson).

Students need to understand that the so-called "first draft" that is submitted to their peers or their teacher for review should not be the first draft they write, but rather the fourth or fifth. In other words, it should be the BEST draft they have been able to write. It is only after writers have finished engaging in internal revision, trying to make the manuscript say what they want it to say, and they have done as much as they can do in externally revising their text, trying to communicate their message to their audience, that they ask a colleague to look over their work, and it is not until after they have revised the manuscript, based on their colleague's remarks, that they finally submit their work to an editor. By the time writers submit a manuscript to their editors, they have written as well as they can.

The truth is that few editors see themselves as writers' collaborators; the Maxwell Perkinses (Perkins was the editor for such writers as Ernest Hemingway, F. Scott Fitzgerald, and Thomas Wolfe) are few and far between. Like all of us who must read students' papers, editors prefer manuscripts that are already done well. The less they have to do to, the happier they are. Students need to learn to expend the effort necessary to complete a paper themselves. If we can assume the role of editors, providing assistance only when we know students cannot handle a certain aspect of the writing because they have not learned how, then we can begin to help students assume responsibility for their own writing processes.

Because in college classes in the content areas, the amount of material to be covered leaves no time for students to work in peer response groups and the instructor has no time to review multiple drafts, students must learn to schedule their writing so that they have time to engage in the revision process and to make the effort to find peers to respond to their papers. As I discussed in Chapter 2, students need to learn to evaluate their own papers, determine the revisions they need to make, and make them.

Collaborating

Ernest Hemingway lamented in his address before the Nobel Prize Committee in 1954 (Baker, 1969, p. 52.), "Writing, at its best, is a lonely life. . . .For [the writer] does his work alone and if he is a good enough writer he must face eternity, or the lack of it, each day." Murray (1968) talks about his feelings of isolation as he writes. "There's just you and the blank page and all that life out there to get a hold on" (230). Writers have always described writing as a solitary activity. However, in the past quarter of a century, discussion has revolved around the concept of writers in collaboration with others: previous writers, teachers, editors, etc. (Gere, 1987). Both of these viewpoints are valid. In fact Murray (1993), in what appears to be a contradictory statement, comments, "Writers shut their door behind them each day, but they are not alone. All the writers, living and dead, whose works they have ever read crowd in the writing room. . . ." (vii). But this concept is a metaphorical one. In truth, the writer sits alone in front of the computer. That first draft can only be written by the writer because only the writer knows what she wants to say. She can consult a thesaurus, she can quote another author, she can contact a friend when she can't think of who the author of the quote is, but she alone decides which word in the thesaurus is appropriate, which quote is the most interesting.

Although co-authors may discuss what they will write prior to actually working on a draft, they do not collaborate during that first drafting phase. I've collaborated on proposals, articles, and even books. Sometimes I've written just a portion of a document with the co-authors writing their portions and then all of us collaborating to put the parts together. At other times I've written the entire document and then turned it over to my co-author to add and revise the text to incorporate his ideas. Only once have I ever sat down with a co-author and written a piece together. All of the other times, I have written my text alone and have written it as well as I could before giving it to my collaborator. Students must understand that writing is not only hard work but also a lonely activity.

Developing Voices

Students have become especially concerned with developing their own voice during the last decade. Ashley (2001) reports that students feel they have to suppress themselves, that they do not have an "individual voice" when they write academic prose. She cites one student who perceived the objective and abstract voice she adopted for writing papers as "self removal" (510). We need to help students realize that just as they have different oral voices, depending on the situation, they also different written voices. The voice they use in a scientific paper is expected to be "voiceless"; it follows a convention established by that community. However, a paper in freshman composition can assume a variety of appropriate voices. Note the different voices in the following examples.

Students wrote these essays for the 2001 NCTE Achievement Awards in Writing as part of a timed writing exercise. The prompt asks students to assume that they have been invited to submit an article about Heroes/Heroines of the New Millennium to the school's newspaper.

(1) If I could pick anyone in the world to be my personal hero, it would have to be. . .well, I can't decide, but I've narrowed it down to George Bush, Pamela Anderson, or my Aunt Judy (who also happens to be my math teacher). I suppose that these people aren't the first people who come to mind when you think of a hero, but by today's standards of heroism, they aren't that far off. In fact, if you want to know what makes a hero in the new millennium, just pick up a copy of your local newspaper. . . .

(2) Hercules! Hercules! Hercules! This chant, which many a grade-schooler will immediately recognize, comes from the popular Disney movie about the ancient hero. Hercules has long been seen as a hero—from the Greeks in 500 B.C. to 90's cool kids. But Hercules was, let's face it, all brawn and no brain. He was clever: that trick with the Hydra was no mean feat, and he certainly knew his way around women, but are these the qualities we want in a modern-day hero? Frankly, I think not. I haven't seen any mythological monsters around, and most women today want the smart guy rather than the easy-come, easy-go type of man. . .

(3) In American society, children are brought up to believe that a hero is one who slays dragons, rescues damsels, saves the day. As children grow into adulthood, this definition matures and develops. Society dictates what is or what is not heroism, depending on the crises a civilization currently faces. When England faced its "darkest hour" as Hitler's third Reich hovered over Europe, the Queen and her citizens turned to Winston Churchill, a warrior and statesman, to lead them to victory. . . . A hero must reflect the grandest dreams and ambitions of the society he or she is a product of. . .

Each of these writers has assumed a special voice for this particular essay, and each voices indicates its own particular individualism. Given a different topic, the writers may have assumed different voices. The chapters in this book reflect multiple voices, yet each is within the conventions of a textbook.

We need to help students understand that they must develop multiple voices rather than a single voice, that their scientific voice will differ from the voice they use in an essay, and that even that voice will differ from the voice they use to write a letter to a friend about the same topic.

Integrating the Expressive with the Transactional

For students to write in-depth essays in composition classes, literary analyses in literature courses, and reports in content areas, they need to integrate the ideas and facts they are acquiring in their classes with their prior knowledge and experience. Britton et al. (1975) describe this as "contextualizing" objective information, that is, making it one's own by putting it in one's own context. Martin, D'areey, Newton, and Parker (1976) observe that "Unless we are given the opportunity to reconstrue and to assimilate gradually what is new, . . . the information will remain inert. . . . the facts will never be galvanized into life for us (68).

By contextualizing the information they read, students can begin to develop their own unique ideas which, in turn, become new to us, their readers. "In every case. . . the writer has something as well as the information (his own experience, his own thoughts, his own feelings or observations) which is not already known to the teacher or the wider audience for whom he is writing" (Martin et al., 1976, p. 69). Thus, their ideas gain a depth that the simple iteration of facts does not provide.

The following excerpt from an Op Ed column by George Will, one of the most erudite columnists in this country, exemplifies this concept.

> "Curiouser and curiouser," said Alice, who was in Wonderland, although she could have been in Minnesota. The misguided Supreme Court of that state will soon answer to the U.S. Supreme Court, trying to defend the indefensible provision in the state's Code of Judicial Conduct, promulgated by the state court, that pushes campaign regulation, meaning the official supervision of political speech, to new levels of offensiveness.
>
> Like a sizable majority of states, Minnesota elects judges, which is a bad idea, but historically understandable. The state Constitution mandating this was adopted on the eve of the Civil War, when abolitionist feelings were running high and so was resentment of the judicial highhandedness that produced the 1857 Dred Scott case.
>
> —George Will
> *The Times,* Hammond, Indiana,
> January 3, 2002, p. A6

Will has written a "contextualized" transactional essay. It presents an expressive view of some factual information. By taking new information about the voting regulations of Minnesota and connecting it to information he already knows about the history of that particular regulation and about similar regulations in other states, he arrives at a personal conclusion—that the regulation is similar to the illogical rules of Wonderland. When Britton and Martin were suggesting that students needed to incorporate the expressive mode into their written work in order to make the information their own, they were not recommending the personal memoir-style essay that has become prevalent in many classes; rather, they were thinking of essays such as Will's.

Students' prior knowledge and experience need to be validated as the recent literature indicates. However, students must learn to integrate that knowledge and experience with the new knowledge they are acquiring and, thus, develop new perceptions. This is what learning is all about.

One of the ways they can accomplish this synthesis is by dialoging with the authors of the various readings they are assigned as we discussed in a previous section. Structured journal entries that require students to reflect on the relationship between their previous knowledge and experience and the ideas they are reading also guide them in this direction. Given an opportunity to "reflect in solitude" on the concepts presented by the authors they read, students can begin to develop ideas that synthesize the mythological world of Greece, the philosophical arguments of Aristotle and Plato, and the political treatises of Marx, Machiavelli, and Thomas Jefferson with contemporary concepts of diversity, the ethics of the Web, and the definition of evil.

Engaging in the Process

I will not spend much time on the writing process as it has been discussed ad infinitum for the last quarter of a century. However, I want to stress the need to help students internalize the process. In college, instructors in content-area classes, including literature classes, expect students to engage in the process, including the various phases of revision, on their own. Therefore, students must learn not only to engage in the process but also KNOW how to engage in the process. By the time students reach college, they should be able to engage in the writing process without teachers structuring their lessons so that class time is devoted to prewriting, peer conferencing, and revising. Given a two-week period in which to write a paper, students should engage in all of the phases as they write without prompting by an instructor. Thus, as teachers, we need to slowly remove the scaffolding we have created around the process so that students can begin to accept the responsibility for engaging in it. By using forward- and backward-reaching transfer as I discussed in Chapter 2, we can prepare students to work on their own.

Structuring Assignments

By structuring assignments so that students engage in the various heuristics discussed in this chapter, we can prepare them to write successful academic discourse. Such assignments should be open ended and involve multiple sources that reflect both canonical and contemporary texts as well as field sources. They should also involve content areas in addition to literature, and they should be aimed at an academic audience.

Writing is hard work. It is lonely. It is frustrating when it does not work. It can be boring when the same section must be rewritten over and over again. It may even become depressing when it doesn't seem that the text will ever say what it needs to say. It is not this way just for neophytes, students who have just begun to write, but it is this way for writers who have been writing professionally for years. Students need to understand that only by expending the effort and the time necessary can they write effective prose. But if they do, they will find the results completely satisfying.

Sometimes, when I am empty, when words don't come, when I haven't written a single sentence after scribbling whole pages, I collapse on my couch and lie there dazed, bogged in a swamp of despair [. . .]. A quarter of an hour later everything changes; my heart is pounding with joy. Last Wednesday I had to get up and fetch my handkerchief; tears were streaming down my face. I had been moved by my own writing; the emotion I had conceived, the phrase that rendered it, and the satisfaction of having found the phrase—all were causing me to experience the most exquisite pleasure

—(Letter to Louise Colet, 24 April 1852, *The Selected Letters of Gustave Flaubert,* tr. and intro. Francis Steegmuller (New York: Vintage, 1957), 130)

References

Ashley, Hannah. 2001. "Playing the Game: Proficient Working-Class Student Writers' Second Voices." *Research in Teaching English* 35: 493–521.

Baker, Carlos. Ernest Hemingway, 1969. New York: Charles Scribner's Sons.

Boiarsky, C. 1997. *The Art of Workplace English.* Portsmouth, NH: Boynton/Cook.

Boiarsky, Carolyn. 1986. "Writing a Thesis Statement: A Right-Brain Activity." *Activities To Promote Critical Thinking.* Urbana, IL: National Council of Teachers of English.

Britton, James. 1970. *Language and Learning.* Harmondsworth, England: Penguin Books.

Britton, James, et al. 1975. *The Development of Writing Abilities (11–18).* London: Macmillan Enterprises, Ltd.

Ede, Lisa, and Andrea Lunsford. 1984. "Audience Addressed/Audience Evoked: The Role of Audience in Composition Theory and Pedagogy." *College Composition and Communication.* 35: 155–71.

Flaubert, Gustave. 1957. "Letter to Louise Colet, 24 April 1852." *The Selected Letters of Gustave Flaubert,* tr. and intro. Francis Steegmuller, 130. New York: Vintage, 1957.

Gere, Anne R. 1987. *Writing Groups.* Carbondale, IL: Southern Illinois University Press.

Hagemann, Julie. 1999. Unpublished manuscript. Hammond, IN: Purdue University Calumet.

Hull, Glynda. 1985. "Research in Error and Correction." In *Perspectives on Research and Scholarship in Composition,* edited by Ben W. McClelland and Tomothy R. Donovan. New York: Modern Language Association.

Macrorie, Ken. 1970. *Uptaught.* Rochelle Park, NJ: Hayden Book Company, Inc.

Martin, Nancy, Pat D'arcy, Bryan Newton, and Robert Parker. 1976. *Writing and Learning Across the Curriculum,* London, England: Schools Council Publication.

Murray, Donald. 1993. *Read to Write,* 3rd ed. Forth Worth: Harcourt, Brace Jovanovich College Publishers.

Murray, Donald. *A Writer Teaches Writing.* 1968, Boston: Houghton Mifflin Company.

Ray, K. W. 1999. *Wondrous Words: Writers and Writing in the Elementary Classroom,* Urbana, IL: National Council of Teachers of English.

Shaughnessy, Mina P. 1977. *Errors and Expectations.* New York: Oxford University Press.

Smith, Frank. 1984. "Reading Like a Writer." In *Composing and Comprehending,* edited by Julie Jensen. Urbana, IL: National Council of Teachers of English.

Van Nostrand, A. D., Charles Knoblauch, and Joan Pettigrew. 1982. *The Process of Writing: Discovery and Control,* 2nd ed. Boston: Houghton Mifflin.

Vygotsky, Lev. 1962. *Thought and Language.* Cambridge, MA: MIT Press.

4

The Work of Composition

Helping Students Mix Function and Art To Become Carpenters and Poets

Steve Fox

Any work, you kneel down—it's a kind of worship. It's part of the holiness of things, work, yes. . . .It's good and not so good. . . .I say my calling is to be a carpenter and a poet. No contradiction.
　　　　　　　—Nick Lindsay, from Studs Terkel's Working

Like Nick Lindsay, as teachers of writing, we are both carpenters and poets in our first-year composition classes. Or more precisely, we teach our students both the craft and the art of writing. As carpenters we teach formal, thesis-based, academic writing. We teach students how to craft academic prose, "working prose," we might call it. They have to make their writing work for them in course after course, semester after semester. We have to help our students use the tools of writing effectively, and though we may fear this is a "functionalist" approach to literacy, it is not. At least, not in a bad way. Assignments that ask students to reflect on significant experiences in their lives, to analyze the way advertising works, to analyze the way a text makes meaning, to construct new meaning out of a response to a text, and to synthesize observations and ideas drawn from focused research steer students toward a literacy that is far richer than mere "functionalism." Such writing can be used for powerful acts of literacy.

As artists we teach the voice, style, and beauty of language. When I think of the students whose writing I have most enjoyed in first-year composition, it is those students whose voices stick with me. Their writing blends genres and voices. They pull in material from an astonishing array of sources: poetry by Carl Sandburg and Robert Service, song lyrics, the Bible, historical and philosophical texts, personal experience. Yet these students' writing is sometimes awkward, confusing, plagiarized, inconsistent, and error-ridden. No matter how much we appreciate the strong voice in such writing or the great potential there, we do not want to "send them into job interviews wearing mismatched clothes," to use a favorite analogy of writing instructors. ("Editing is important; you wouldn't want to go into a job interview with a stain on your tie.") True, we do not grumble as loudly about the textual errors and mishaps of students who write analytical, interesting prose. But we cannot neglect helping all our students acquire a grasp of organizational, stylistic, and grammatical strategies. An apprentice wants to work alongside someone who will show him not only how to make beautiful carvings for furniture but also how to use a hammer, nails, saw, and wood to build the frames for those shelves, doors, and tables. Nor does an apprentice want to listen to endless philosophizing about the ultimate use of those items and their potential for inappropriate purposes—whether a shelf might be used to store pornographic literature, or a door to keep people out of a public space, or a table to eat tasteless, unhealthy food. Rather an apprentice wants to know how to turn the lathe, how to change its angle, how to shape a large piece without splitting it.

Our challenge with most students in first-year college composition is to help them use the tools needed to succeed in an academic setting for the next several years, while also helping them appreciate how those tools can help them work well and live well long after college is a fond memory. We English teachers love language and believe that reading and writing are wonderful tools that human beings acquire. Because we work in the academy, we may have trouble remembering at times that reading and writing occur outside the ivied (or bare concrete) walls we inhabit, but most of us recognize the glories of reading for pleasure (even mystery, romance, and espionage novels), reading for practical information (how to buy a new car, how to fix a leaky pipe), reading for civic engagement (newspapers, magazines, pamphlets, Web sites, petitions), as well as writing for all these purposes. So while we are helping our students learn to write thesis-based, synthetic papers, we also want them to develop writing purposes and processes that will sustain them beyond the baccalaureate.

Our Purpose?

This book argues that our primary purpose is to help students attain academic literacy, the kinds of literacy needed to succeed in earning an undergraduate degree. But given the range of degree programs and the diverse goals of our students, this answer needs elucidating. Many of our students will never go to graduate school and thus not be engaged in academic literacy most of their lives, so we need to offer a more long-term literacy. Should that be workforce literacy? personal literacy? civic literacy? public literacy?

Let me pause here to summarize briefly some of the discussion going on in our field today about the purposes for teaching writing. C. H. Knoblauch (1990) summarizes four of the most common: (1) literacy "for professional competence in a technological world," or functionalist literacy; (2) literacy "for civic responsibility and the preservation of heritage," or cultural literacy; (3) literacy "for personal growth and self-fulfillment"; and (4) literacy "for social and political change," or critical literacy (75–79). Knoblauch insists, as do many literacy theorists, that each approach to or definition of literacy is laden with the values of its proponents and can become a means to control others. Functionalist approaches to literacy might claim to be value-neutral, to simply offer people skills they can use for their own purposes, but Knoblauch argues that functionalist literacy "safeguards the socioeconomic status quo" (76) and often supports "a social program that maintains managerial classes— whose members are always more than just functionally literate—in their customary places while outfitting workers with the minimal reading and writing skills needed for usefulness to the modern information economy" (76–77). Cultural literacy proponents, such as E. D. Hirsch, claim to be offering opportunity to the disadvantaged, for no one can succeed in a society without having access to cultural as well as economic capital. Yet Knoblauch notes the melancholy nostalgia of many cultural literacy arguments: the language is being corrupted, a once pure society is turning into a tower of Babel (77). Pundits of different ideological stripes lament that young people do not know who the Founding Fathers are, that they do not know the Founding Mothers either, that they have no idea on what principles our nation is founded, and that U.S. history and literature are taught as simplistic narratives of progress, or decline and fall. As for liberal proponents of the personal growth approach, Knoblauch notes they can be co-opted by the system; their goal of moderate reform is less threatening to school boards and politicians than truly radical, institutional change (78).

Knoblauch clearly favors the fourth purpose, critical literacy, the one that draws on the work of Brazilian educator and social activist Paulo Freire. As Knoblauch defines this approach, its purpose is "to identify reading and writing abilities with a critical consciousness of the social conditions in which people find themselves. . . . Literacy, therefore, constitutes a means to power, a way to seek political enfranchisement . . . . At stake, from this point of view, is, in principle, the eventual reconstituting of the class structure of American life, specifically a change of those capitalist economic practices that assist the dominance of particular groups" (79). Freire's adult literacy work in the Third World has been widely applauded by some academics and educators in the United States. Yet most of us in this country are not working with the kinds of basic literacy education or adult working-class students that Freire worked with. Knoblauch notes that Freirean professors draw their income and social status from the prevailing system, and for this and other reasons he seems skeptical of the radical potential of this movement in the United States.

Each of these arguments for literacy could be examined and debated at great length. [If you are interested, you can read Berlin (1987), Bloom, Daiker, and White (1996), and Gradin (1995), but as this is not the focus for this book I will not go into them here.] I agree that we must question the ultimate goals of our educational system and our own teaching philosophies. And Knoblauch is right to ask all educators to critique our own philosophy and our tendency to colonize students with our values. But I come back to everyday reality and pragmatism; I suppose that's the liberal American tradition from which I work. I see that major structural changes are needed to ensure "liberty and justice for all." I want my students to know the radical possibilities of their cultural library: the Declaration of Independence, the Bill of Rights, the Gettysburg Address, the U.N. Charter, and texts by writers as diverse as Frederick Douglass, Eugene Debs, Charlotte Perkins Gilman, and Martin Luther King. But I also know that students cannot appreciate the power of these texts without some sort of "functional" literacy—an ability to read, write, and analyze language. They also need cultural, and multicultural, literacy to understand the range of references in these powerful texts. Whether a student needs or wants personal growth or communal change—whether I as a teacher see my classroom as a space for individual or group liberation—some sort of "critical" literacy is required. My goal remains to have students respond critically to texts and experiences, and to develop thoughtful ways of arriving at a thesis and using supporting evidence—or, in the case of autobiographical writing, to develop the kinds of literary techniques used by good nonfiction writers to investigate the world.

Our Approach?

Given this purpose, what should the approach to composition instruction be? When I see my students through the lens of socioeconomic class, when I consider their working-class backgrounds or working-class status and activity, I cannot help but question whether I should change my curriculum or my pedagogy to adapt to this image as some educators have recommended, such as James Zebroski, Julie Lindquist, and Linda Adler-Kassner. In short, what difference does being working class (or not) make to students and to me as their teacher in first-year composition? If being "working class" means for many students that they are not well-read, not widely read, and not inclined to put their thoughts and feelings and perceptions into written form, then it makes a difference. It is hard for students to weave an intertextual web when they have few texts to pull strands from. It is hard for them to adapt their writing style to academic constraints when they have little experience writing at all. Of course, working-class students are sometimes avid readers and writers, as I have found. In those cases, they may face conflicts between their literacy practices and family and community values.[1] And students from middle-class, professional homes can be "a-literate," but at least in their homes and schools, formal, school-based literacy is at hand, is supported, even if it isn't always truly appreciated.

The Curriculum

So what do we do? How can our literacy instruction help working-class students attain or even broaden their goals?

Content

One answer to this question has been to offer students the opportunity to share their experiences and to reflect on what it means to be working class in a school or university and in this society. We can offer readings that highlight and represent working-class voices to help working-class students gain a greater understanding of their own class and thereby a greater respect for themselves by having them read and write about being working class. But I am not sure we have the right to require students to use specific kinds of experiences or to reflect on such matters. What right have we to satisfy our curiosity, meet our research objectives, or practice our political ideology without their consent? We can certainly create a comfortable environment for honest discussion and personal reflection—but we can't create an entirely safe environment without remaking our whole society. We can ask students to think about class-related issues, but we should not push them to do so in a particular way. If they want to write or think about something else or adopt a "new" identity and perspective, that is their right and privilege. But we should not assume that any of our students, including working-class students, need us to teach them self-respect or respect for their family and community. Perhaps some of us as educators are being patronizing and are the ones who need to learn respect for the "working class."

Whether or not we adopt a pedagogy that specifically focuses on working-class students, we can design a curriculum that helps all students acquire both the craft and the art of composition. I have found that a theme-based curriculum that uses a seminar-style class and that provides assignments that involve students in synthesizing various sources of information can be effective.

About five years ago, I worked with my colleagues in the Writing Program at IU/PUI (Indiana University/Purdue University Indianapolis) to develop a composition curriculum centered on the theme of work. Prior to that I had worked with a theme-centered curriculum at University of Wisconsin-Madison, where we had focused on literacy.[2] I find working with a theme-based curriculum is a good way to involve my students in deep critical thinking because they have an opportunity to spend time considering a subject in many ways from differing points of view. Having learned how important a role work and working played in IU/PUI students' lives, I suggested to my writing program colleagues a seminar focused on the topic of work. The "subject" of writing classes would still be writing, but the "subjects" of students' reading and writing would be work-related in some broad way. My colleagues embraced this idea readily, and we wrote a curriculum that in many ways underlies our present curriculum, even though we have moved on to other themes— first to literacy and education and recently to a more book-centered, less thematic approach (with books as diverse as Jon Krakauer's *Into the Wild,* Jon Katz's *Geeks,* and Helen Prejean's *Dead Man Walking*). However, we still use a seminar model and similar types of assignments.

The nontraditional students—the ones who have been out of school for several years, or many years, and have identified themselves primarily by their jobs, not by their status as students or teenagers—identify most with work issues and often write best about these topics. Some of them, and many of our younger, traditional students, tire of the work theme, or do not want to write about work when it occupies so much of their lives already. But we face this with any subject and any book we use, so I don't see it as a major problem. I would like to do another writing class focused on work, perhaps linked with a course on the sociology of work, or the history of work.

Readings

I prefer to use trade books (books published for general audiences, not as textbooks) rather than anthologies for a number of reasons. First of all, the selections in these readers are lifted from their original contexts, often with little explanation of those contexts, and sometimes are edited or shortened. Original documentation, especially bibliographies, is usually not included. Students opening such readers are faced with a bewildering smorgasbord of pop social science, literary nonfiction, magazine and newspaper editorializing, and occasionally some token bits from academic journals. No argument, no tone or perspective, is sustained for more than a few pages.

Thus, for my course I try to find a nonfiction trade book that raises a range of interesting issues related to the theme. Students have at least the immediate context of the writer's ideas (the book cover, any introductory matter, the full text, footnotes, and references), and it is possible for even a busy composition instructor to provide other contextual matter (or ask students to search for it), in a way that would be impossible for a reader with fifty or more selections.

Whatever the pros and cons of individual books, I remain committed to the nonfiction trade book. Because such books are the mainstay of most people's reading and because our English classes focus so heavily on fiction, we who teach writing have much to gain from using nonfiction books as a springboard for analytical writing. One feature of the new Indiana Department of Education state reading list is a greater emphasis on nonfiction. Giving students a readable, yet thoughtful and weighty contemporary nonfiction trade book is a good way to promote critical, lifelong literacy.

I began teaching this course using Juliet Schor's *The Overworked American*. Schor is an academic economist, but she is writing in this book for a larger audience. (In fact, she has been quoted in newspapers and magazines and made the talk-show circuit at times.) She presents a clear, strong thesis in her book, one that is arguable in terms of quantitative data, historical perspective, values, and comparative culture. I think *The Overworked American* offers rich material for students to practice summarizing, responding analytically, and pursuing related questions of their own. But many students have difficulties with *The Overworked American,* or at least tire of it over the course of fifteen weeks (perhaps we ended up with the overworked thesis), and in response to their strident complaints over two semesters, I (along with the rest of our first-year composition instructors) switched to Studs Terkel's book of interviews, *Working.* Everyone enjoys reading this book. Terkel gives working-class people a voice, and lets working-class students (among others) see their experiences in a text. As bell hooks (1999) points out, working-class people are not well represented in published texts:

> No one speaks about class and the politics of writing in this society. It is just assumed that everyone has equal opportunity when it comes to writing and publishing. Taken seriously such an assumption seems ludicrous, given the reality that so many citizens of our nation do not read or write and that most of what is published comes from an educated elite who are either from privileged class backgrounds or are aspiring to enter privileged classes. (97)

Working, however, has its problems. Terkel is not arguing a thesis, though his own perspectives on work are presented in a delightful, yet rambling introduction. The book is a written version of oral speech, so it must be analyzed and used differently from a book like Schor's. And one of the major complaints against it is that it does not provide an example of academic writing. Of course, this seeming deficit can be turned into a virtue. Zebroski (1990) uses texts like Terkel's *Working* precisely because they "blur boundaries and speak many languages" (85). And some instructors in our program at IU/PUI liked Terkel's book because it did not set forth an explicit thesis, but instead pushed students to analyze the various perspectives voiced in the book and develop their own theses.

Assignments

The assignments in the work curriculum asked students to look at work, both from their own and others' perspectives. We had students interview someone about their work and turn the interview write-ups into another class text. Students wrote their first or second essay as an autobiographical narrative about work; these essays served as primary sources or as springboards for thesis-based essays. Another assignment used by some instructors was a field experience essay. This assignment asked students to write about a workplace or work-related issue, doing firsthand research—often interviews, but sometimes observation or firsthand experience, supplemented with limited library research. Another assignment requires students to analyze the way *work* is represented in some form of media: an advertisement, a television show, a movie, a children's book, a popular song. (Our revised curriculum at IU/PUI continues to have similar assignment options, including an analytical response to the reading, an autobiographical narrative, and analysis of images such as print ads.)

Among my own faculty, I have engaged in several vigorous debates about using a narrative assignment in a curriculum that aims primarily at helping students develop an analytical, thesis-based writing style, the kind of writing that will best serve them in other courses. Although faculty acknowledge that students enjoy the narrative assignment, and some of them also enjoy reading it (I do; it's my favorite part of the semester), they point out that writing good literary narrative is difficult and is hard to teach in only one assignment; we have other courses—creative writing, literary nonfiction, literary journalism—that focus on that form. However, I believe narrative can be a powerful component of analytical writing and that perhaps we need to teach our students how to do this. Our rhetoric in first-semester composition, Ramage and Bean's *The Allyn and Bacon Guide to Writing,* presents a stylistic range from open-form to closed-form prose. The autobiographical narrative paper is at the open-form end of this continuum, and a highly formal, thesis-based essay (such as our assignment that asks students to respond analytically to a section of their nonfiction trade book) is at the closed-form end. We are trying harder to show students how good writing can move up and down this continuum. We know it is most advantageous to wield prose as a flexible tool, to be able to move from a highly constrained genre into multi-genre and open-form texts. [I'm not sure I agree with Zebroski (1990) that *working-class* students prefer such blurred genres, such open-ended texts.] But we are also aware that it is not easy to write such prose if one cannot write formal essays with a more linear design. Thus, I try to provide students a scaffold by using a more developmental approach, helping them find where they are on that continuum and then helping them move further along it.

Last semester, my first-year composition course was one of several linked with introductory sociology, and the nonfiction book my students read and wrote about in both composition and sociology was Helen Prejean's *Dead Man Walking.* One of Prejean's major discoveries, one that my students made with her assistance, was that class, like "race" or color, has a tremendous amount to do with who receives the death penalty. I'm not sure how much we connected that realization with our own lives, class identities, or literacies. I believe some students began making at least implicit connections. Cheyenne, a single mother who had read voraciously and thirsted to know more about history, philosophy, religion, and politics, wrote her four papers as four sections of a personal investigation into religion and politics. In her autobiographical narrative, she wrote about what she had learned during a custody battle with her ex-husband—she realized that *what* she knew could trump *who* her ex-husband, his lawyer, and the judge knew. She used literacy to understand the family courts and the justice system and won back her son. Cheyenne could have looked at how her story differed from those of the death-row prisoners Prejean writes about, and class could have been one variable in that equation. Another student, also a single mother, wrote about her family's gaining firsthand knowledge of the criminal justice system when her brother was arrested, charged with drug possession, and sentenced to a surprisingly long term by a judge determined to make an example of him.

Steve, another of my students, also made the connection between his life and the lives we were reading. But he made other connections, too: between past and present, art and techne, his prior knowledge and the new knowledge he was gaining. Steve was the first member of his immediate family to go to college. Although Steve's grandfather had become wealthy through a number of businesses he owned in Indianapolis, he had no more than an eighth-grade education. Steve's father, plagued by personal problems, did not do so well and eventually left his family. Steve's mother found a job with the state government, where she still works. Despite this background, Steve was able to attend a prestigious suburban high school and thus received a good college-preparatory education. However, he did not go directly to college, but instead worked in a small town as a meter reader, where he kept his walkman tuned in to National Public Radio instead of a commercial music station and could be found reading a book when he wasn't walking the streets. When Steve decided to go to college—he wanted to be a high school English teacher—he came, like many nontraditional students, to IU/PUI. He was in my first-year composition class when we were using *Working*. When it came time to write an analytical response to one of the interviews in Terkel, Steve chose to write about Nick Lindsay, the philosophical, even spiritual, carpenter–poet whom Terkel found in northern Indiana. Steve begins his paper this way:

> Plato once said, "Philosophy is the highest music." Well that sounds intellectual enough; but I disagree. I think that philosophy is country music, or at least it should be. The common person cannot hear the highest music, it's only heard by those that can afford to think all day. But country music is real, it wears a blue-collar, and it is practical. The man that swings the hammer can think, he can philosophize, and he can speak on spiritual terms about his niche in the world. [See the Appendix at the end of this chapter for the full text of Steve's essay.]

Throughout the piece, Steve cites such writers as Don Quixote, Will Rogers, Gordon Lightfoot, Bill Monroe, the Apostle Paul, and Robert Service, from the shelves of his cultural library. Steve connects his personal experience with Terkel's text, and he juxtaposes high culture and popular culture. He has written analytical, organized prose that is also critical, interesting prose, and he has enclosed his ideas in the techniques of good literary writers to create vivid images of his world. He has become both a craftsman and a poet.

Ironically, in this essay I focus on working-class students in an institution—the university—that has usually been seen as a way out of the working class. Yet students like Steve remind us that class categories, like other labels applied to people, resist easy definition and simple application to any individual. Educators and students together can investigate what it means to be working class in our society, and through that inquiry create opportunities for people to celebrate their working-class origins and identity and accomplish their goals. Listening to the words of working-class students, helping them build bridges between their personal literacies and academic literacy, encouraging them to make their mark on the page and perhaps thereby on the world—that is our work, our art, and our craft.

Notes

1. See Muldoon's amusing take on this in his "My Turn" essay in *Newsweek,* "White-Collar Man in Blue-Collar World." Also see Yagelski (2000, pp. 20–8) and any of the collections of autobiographies by working-class academics, such as the one edited by Dews and Law (1995).

2. For a full account of the UW-Madison curriculum, see Weese, Fox, and Greene (1999).

References

Adler-Kassner, Linda. 1999. "The Shape of the Form: Working-Class Students and the Academic Essay." In *Teaching Working Class,* edited by S. L. Linkon, pp. 85–105. Amherst: University of Massachusetts.

Berlin, James A. 1987. *Rhetoric and Reality: Writing Instruction in American Colleges, 1900-* Carbondale: Southern Illinois UP, 1987.

Bloom, Lynn Z., Donald A. Daiker, and Edward M. White, eds. 1996. *Composition in the Twenty-First Century: Crisis and Change.* Carbondale: Southern Illinois UP.

Dews, C.L. Barney, and Carolyn Leste Law, eds. 1995. *This Fine Place So Far From Home: Voices of Academics from the Working Class.* Philadelphia: Temple UP.

Gradin, Sherrie L. 1995. *Romancing Rhetorics: Social Expressivist Perspectives on the Teaching of Writing.* Portsmouth, NH: Boynton/Cook.

hooks, bell. 1999. "Class and the Politics of Writing." *Remembered Rapture: The Writer at Work,* New York: Holt. pp. 97–107.

Knoblauch, C. H. 1990. "Literacy and the Politics of Education." In *The Right to Literacy,* edited by A. A. Lunsford, H. Moglen, and J. Slevin, pp. 74–80. New York: MLA.

Linkon, Sherry Lee, ed. 1999. *Teaching Working Class.* Amherst: University of Massachusetts.

Lunsford, Andrea A., Helene Moglen, and James Slevin, eds. 1990. *The Right to Literacy.* New York: MLA.

Muldoon, Bob. "White-Collar Man in a Blue-Collar World." *Newsweek* 4 (February 2002): 13.

Schor, Juliet B. 1991. *The Overworked American: The Unexpected Decline of Leisure.* New York: Basic Books.

Terkel, Studs. 1994. *Working: People Talk About What They Do All Day and How They Feel About What They Do.* New York: The New Press.

Weese, Katherine L., Stephen L. Fox, and Stuart Greene. 1999. *Teaching Academic Literacy: The Uses of Teacher-Research in Developing a Writing Program.* Mahwah, NJ: Erlbaum.

Yagelski, Robert P. 2000. *Literacy Matters: Writing and Reading the Social Self.* New York: Teachers College Press.

Zebroski, James Thomas. 1990. "The English Department and Social Class: Resisting Writing." In *The Right to Literacy,* edited by A. A. Lunsford, H. Moglen, and J. Slevin, pp. 81–7. New York: MLA.

Appendix
Building a Philosophy out of Words and Wood by Steve Skirvin

He is so common as to be uncommon.

—Ray Bradbury

Plato once said, "Philosophy is the highest music." Well that sounds intellectual enough; but I disagree. I think that philosophy is country music, or at least it should be. The common person cannot hear the highest music, it's only heard by those that can afford to think all day. But country music is real, it wears a blue collar, and it is practical. The man that swings the hammer can think, he can philosophize, and he can speak on spiritual terms about his niche in the world. Just listen to what common man Nick Lindsay says: "A man, if he describes himself, will use a verb. What you do, that's what you are. I would say I'm a carpenter" (670). Sound philosophy coming from a man with calloused hands. I doubt if Plato had a single callous on his hands.

A man once said, "Blessed is he that has found his work, and let him ask no other blessedness." Nick Lindsay has found his work in carpentry and writing poetry, building things with words and wood. "I say my calling is to be a carpenter and a poet. No contradiction" (674). Lindsay has considered and accepted his calling. He looked down his family tree, and saw that Lindsays have been doing carpentry since the eighteenth century. He learned to drive nails, and saw boards at the age of thirteen, and his education has continued right up into adulthood. "You can learn a lot from books about things like this; how nails work, different kinds of wood," Lindsay says concerning his continuing vocational education. After reading Lindsay reflect on his job, and how it relates to the state of affairs around him, it's easy to imagine him tacking shingles on a roof while at the same time reading *Don Quixote;* equally at home with roofing nails and seventeenth-century literature. He wields his hammer much like Gordon Lightfoot wields his guitar, with firsthand experience and thoughtful observation. Normal carpenters don't speak of, nor in a zillion years would they consider, the "creative mystery" that the woods they use are a part of. "Each wood has its own spirit. Driving nails, yeah, your spirit will break against that" (670). Lindsay talking about driving nails and his spirit breaking sounds similar to Will Rogers expounding on the virtues of cow punching; it's downright moving.

Lindsay, speaking on spiritual terms about work, says, "It's a kind of worship" (671). He uses the example of a man kneeling down to wire up an organ in a church to illustrate his idea of work as worship. In this concept, Lindsay echoes the words of the Apostle Paul, who wrote, "With good will doing service, as to the Lord, and not to men . . . " (Ephesians 6:7). I am reminded of an old Bill Monroe song: "I'm working on a building, I'm working on a building, For my Lord, for my Lord." Lindsay continues along these lines: "It's part of the holiness of things, work, yes. Just like drawing breath is. It's necessary. If you don't breathe, you're dead" (671).

"It's good not to push too hard," says Lindsay. He's right; the number of on-the-job accidents could be greatly reduced if folks would just slow down. One should savor each moment, and rest assured that break time will roll around pretty soon. Some old Roman emperor said it best when he said, "Make haste slowly."

Just like hammering nails into a house, Lindsay considers writing poetry a natural act. "It's the natural utterance of a living language" (674). Because he writes poems, he doesn't consider himself to be any better than those who don't. Poetry doesn't work that way for him. Just like his carpentry skills, his poetry writing skills are practical. If you needed something, you could just as natural and easy say, "Hey, Nick, I need five-eighths cut off this stud," or "Hey, Nick, I need a poem about those Canadian geese that just flew over." It wouldn't matter to Lindsay; it's all part of his calling.

After studying Nick Lindsay for a while, you could probably tell me that he jumped off the pages of some novel somewhere and entered the world. To me, he is a special person. I've been around carpenters, I've even done a little carpentry work myself, and I have always wondered why you don't come across more Nick Lindsay types in that line of work. I mean, after all, Jesus was at one time a carpenter. A shame more folks don't consider the impact of their lives and the work they do. Instead of closing out this paper with some clever wording, I want to give one of my favorite poets the last word concerning Nick Lindsay and those like him. And it seemed natural when writing about Lindsay to end with a poem, so here it is.

> We plug away and make no fuss,
> Our feats are never crowned;
> And yet it's common coves like us
> Who make the world go round,

And as we steer a steady course
By God's predestined plan,
Hat's off to that mighty force:
THE ORDINARY MAN.
          —Robert Service (The final stanza of his poem, "The Ordinary Man")

Works Cited

Terkel, Studs. 1974. *Working.* NY: Ballantine Books.
The Bible. 1982. New King James Version. NY: American Bible Society.
Service, Robert. 1953. *The Best of Robert Service.* NY: Dodd, Mead, and Co.

5

Challenging But Safe Environments

Helping Students Succeed in College Writing

Kelly Belanger and Diane Panozzo

In this chapter, we draw upon our students' own words and our combined thirty-nine years of working with high school and first-year college students to suggest ways high school and college writing teachers can create classroom environments that encourage students from all class backgrounds, but especially from the working class, to take the risks necessary for academic success. Our aim is to imagine learning environments in which students do not simply "play the game," focusing on filling up the required number of pages to meet requirements and get their work "out of the way." Our hope is for students to experience what Sondra Perl (1980) terms a "felt sense" of writing, what psychologists call "flow" (Csikszentmihalyi, 1991),[1] and what Cheyenne East High School student Jenelle Ley calls "a living and breathing thing" (interview, December 6, 2001).

We asked ourselves what it is that we need to do in high school and college writing classes to enable students to engage in these experiences. To find the answer, we reviewed much of the literature during the past decade and then interviewed many of our present students along with a number of former students who have gone on to institutions of higher education, ranging from the local community college to Stanford and Princeton universities. We concluded that we needed to provide classrooms that "stretched" our students by (1) insisting on active learning, (2) maintaining high expectations (in part by making explicit connections between high school and college standards for writing), and (3) fostering the intrinsic value of learning. But we also recognized that we needed to help our students, especially our working-class students, acquire confidence in themselves to meet these ambitious goals. Thus, it was incumbent upon us to create a "safe" environment in which to guide our students through new intellectual challenges as well as the anxieties and insecurities that accompany them to college.

Creating a Safe Environment

It's easy to forget how quickly students can be intimidated into silence, can retreat into a perfunctory process that only resembles learning. During our interviews, Diane's AP students emphasized the need for teachers to deal with "the intimidation factor." According to one of her most capable AP students, when the class was first faced with the challenge of writing their own ideas on the spot and then sharing them with their peers, "everyone almost dropped AP." A first-year college student in Kelly's fall semester writing course wrote in retrospect about the first weeks of class, "Entering a new environment for the first time, feeling the curiosity of others as they watched as I walked into the quiet room. The first day of classes is always scary and sometimes uninviting. I didn't know what I had gotten myself into" (final exam, Morgan Amberson, December 13, 2000).

Although these students do not connect their need for an inviting environment to their socioeconomic class backgrounds, Deborah Mutnick, author of *Writing in an Alien World,* does as she looks back on her own entry into a college environment. She describes her silence, fear, and sense of being overwhelmed "because of a disparity between [her] assumption of entitlement as a middle-class person and her discovery that [she] was ignorant of social codes that other, more privileged freshman seemed to know intimately" (1996, xviii).

For working-class students, the contrast between the language, expectations, and culture of the university and their home cultures can be even more significant. They need a way to bridge these two cultures.

John Dewey first articulated the need to draw from students' community and cultural identities as a way to help them move from one culture to another in the 1930s.

> A primary responsibility of educators is that they not only be aware of the general principle of the shaping of actual experience by environing conditions, but that they also recognize in the concrete what surroundings are conducive to having experiences that lead to growth. . . . The school environment of desks, blackboards, a small school yard, was supposed to suffice. [In traditional education,] there was no demand that the teacher should become intimately acquainted with the conditions of the local community, physical, historical, economic, occupational, etc., in order to utilize them as educational resources. (1938, pp. 39–40)

We agree with Dewey that it is a worthy goal to create an environment to which students and teachers can bring all their experiences and cultures, their knowledge and understanding, their hopes, their fears, their lack of awareness, and their questions so that a bridge can be constructed between these known cultures and the new culture of the academy.

The Student Academic Center at Indiana University has attempted to create such a bridge in a course aimed at teaching critical analysis and research. In describing his curriculum, Joseph Heathcott invites students to discuss their anxieties about speaking "properly" in college. Opening a discussion of what it means to communicate appropriately in both home and school contexts, he attempts to raise consciousness about the code-switching we all do in different situations where different communication styles are valued (1999).

Heathcott's curriculum mirrors a first-year course at UW designed for provisionally admitted students. The curriculum at both universities begins with analyses of the familiar (students' hometowns at UW; popular rap music at Indiana). Next students analyze less familiar texts (*Our America,* by Jones and Newman (1998), a nonfiction book about challenges faced by an African-American community in Chicago at UW; Philip S. Foner's *We, The Other People* (1976) a collection of declarations of independence from American social movements at Indiana). Students then move on to analyzing more diverse and complex texts that illustrate multiple interpretations (a series of paired texts that illustrate forms of argument from a variety of authors and genres at UW; Godfrey Reggio and Philip Glass' film *Koyaanisqatsi* at Indiana). Finally, students move from analysis to research-based argument. This gradual movement to increasingly complex analysis seems crucial in helping students, who are more practiced in summarizing and reporting, make the transition to college writing.

Encouraging Active Learning

To guide students toward active learning, we need to help them assume responsibility for their own education. We can do so by showing them how to participate in a conference on a draft, to ask specific questions of the instructor and their peers, and to use a handbook to answer some of their own questions about punctuation and grammar.

In our experience, the most effective teachers of writing:

- Listen and try to understand each student, paying equal attention to *all* students (as much as it is possible to do this in a class period)
- Insist that students listen to and respect each other
- Have patience and deliberately give their students *time* to digest ideas, experiment with them, explore them, take risks, make mistakes, solve writing problems, and make discoveries
- Encourage the exchange of ideas, stories, questions, thoughts in class interactions
- Dissipate competition between writers, making it clear that writing processes are individual and varied, but that in many contexts, writers can collaborate
- Value *all* writers
- Model writing in the class all the time
- Bring to class their own writing, on occasion

- Take the time to conference
- Allow for and foster differences in their students, treating them as individuals;
- Inspire action in their students, letting them know they will have to read in class almost every day *whatever* they write—poor or fabulous or mediocre—and therefore, they must have done the writing the night before. The lesson: preparation is expected in this class
- Work together with individuals and the whole class, not singling out the same students day after day
- Give diplomatic but honest feedback and criticism, not caving in to avoid hurting someone's feelings

In pursuit of these good practices, here are some questions we might ask ourselves, not allowing ourselves excuses, not blaming students, but critically examining what really happens each day in our classrooms:

- Do we allow *all* students to participate in discussions?
- Do we teach to our audience (the students)?
- Do we listen to our students' voices? Do we know who these students are and where they are from and what they know?
- Have we given them an entry reading and writing inventory (a list of questions about reading and writing experiences over the years)? Have you made up one yourself and taken the inventory yourself?
- Do we think about the context in which we are teaching and the purpose of our teaching this very day?
- Do we problem-pose and assess students' needs?
- How do we listen for students' hidden voices? (In problem-posing, unlike other competency-based approaches, the "needs assessment" is not completed before the beginning of class, nor is the listening effort undertaken by the teacher alone. As content is drawn from learners' daily lives, listening becomes an ongoing process involving both teachers and students as co-learners and co-explorers) (Wallenstein, 1987, p. 35).
- Have we considered the physical arrangement of desks (ours included) and the visual, tactile, sensory qualities of our rooms? What do our rooms say about us as teachers and as people? Would we want to come to this room each day?
- Are we organized and prepared daily? Do we walk in late? Do we look excited when students walk in our rooms?
- Have we established some routine that students can work inside of without being too rigid?
- Do we allow for surprise, spontaneity, invention, and epiphanies?

Too many questions? Maybe not enough. Reflective teachers ask them-selves these questions each day. Considering these questions, Diane admits that she too frequently rushes into class at the last minute, using traveling from classroom to classroom as her excuse, taking the first minutes of class time to become oriented to the work of the day. Kelly realizes that she relies too much on a point system to make writers accountable for daily writing, when expect-ing students to share and read their writing in each class session would be a more authentic way to signal that she expects students to come prepared for class. Asking these questions of ourselves and of each other keeps us honest, alive, fresh, motivated. Too much to think about? This is the art of teaching, the wonder and joy of solving problems together, exploring ideas we haven't thought of in a certain way before, getting to know each other, learning and questioning, an ongoing process.

Maintaining High Expectations

One of teachers' most important charges is to make students aware, realisti-cally, of the literacy expectations they will face in academia, the world of work, and society in general. Students are not necessarily aware of what level of read-ing and writing will be expected of them at the next stage of their education. Educators, such as Lisa Delpit (1995), have argued strongly for explicit and rigorous teaching of the basic skills to students, arguing that not to do so is to disenfranchise minority and working-class students even further. Others argue for giving working-class students access, through collaborative work, to the so-cial networks and cultural capital of more privileged students (Beech, 2001). As dialogic teachers of writing, part of our contribution to our exchanges with students is to help them see their ways across the bridge between high school and college freshman outcomes in English.[2]

Assessment specialists advise teachers to make a list of what they want students to be able to do at the end of their courses. Last fall, Diane made the following list of outcomes for her senior English class.

Students will be able to:

- Read critically by applying annotation skills in a close reading
- Write critically about a text by examining syntax, diction, metaphor, allit-eration, sentence length, and other literary devices
- Discuss the text with abandon, passion, and intelligence with classmates while taking risks without intimidation
- Read their critical papers to classmates and to us with confidence and without intimidation or embarrassment
- Learn the habit of writing by doing timed writings daily
- Learn the habit of revising by rewriting papers until they get closer to dis-covering what they really wanted to say

- Conference with us and others about their papers
- Listen critically when conferencing
- Write three formal essays each semester
- Learn *how* to write persuasively
- Learn *how* to write reflectively
- Learn *how* to write a rhetorical argument;
- Learn *how* to write a reader-response essay
- Learn *how* to write a formal rhetorical analysis of various texts
- Learn *how* to write a personal essay for college
- Learn *how* to do formal research using technology
- Keep a vocabulary notebook and give a vocabulary presentation
- Demonstrate knowledge of poetic devices, literary devices, rhetorical analysis, rhetorical tropes, grammatical concepts on quizzes
- Teach a class
- To learn to love reading literary books through our modeling a love for reading books in the classroom

Diane then compared her outcomes to the following statement of outcomes for Kelly's first-year writing students at the University of Wyoming that had been adapted from the Council of Writing Project Administrators (WPA) *Outcomes Statement for First-Year Composition*[3] in 2001.

W1: First-Year Writing Outcomes

The following outcomes describe the common knowledge, skills, and habits that Kelly wanted her students to be able to demonstrate by the end of a W1 course.

Rhetorical Knowledge

- Focus on a specific purpose.
- Anticipate the needs of different kinds of readers.
- Recognize the differences among kinds of writing situations.
- Use the conventions of format, organization, and language appropriate to specific writing situations.
- Understand what makes writing types different (such as a personal essay, editorial, or a research report).

Critical Thinking, Reading, and Writing

- Use writing as a vehicle for examining texts and how effectively texts achieve their purposes and address their audiences.

- Find, evaluate, analyze, and synthesize appropriate primary and secondary sources in order to meet the demands of different kinds of writing situations and types of writing.

Composing Processes

- Use a multiple-draft process.
- Use appropriate computer technologies for revision.
- Use collaborative strategies to investigate, write, revise, and edit for a variety of writing situations.

Knowledge of Conventions

- Control general conventions of spelling, grammar, structure, transition, and punctuation expected in standard written English.
- Document primary and secondary sources appropriately.
- Know how to use a handbook to understand conventions that may be unclear.
- Understand that different conventions are appropriate for different kinds of writing situations.

One of Kelly's colleagues outside the English Department commented that these outcomes appeared too idealistic for first-year college students. Many senior English teachers would similarly find Diane's list too ambitious, unattainable even, for the most prepared, motivated students. Indeed when working with students labeled "basic" or with provisionally admitted college students, the full range of these goals may not be possible for most students. Realistically, for each of us, the extent to which these outcomes are met depends on the time we spend preparing, the mix of students and their cultures and experiences, constraints of public education, such as schedules and grades, our openness to change, and our ability to orchestrate and facilitate learning moments as they evolve. Always, too, there is the fact that between "birth and their 19th birthdays American children spend 9 percent of their time in school, 91 percent elsewhere" (Will, 2001). This reality puts in perspective what can be accomplished in school, underlining the importance of educating parents and communities about ways they can supplement and support classroom work. Even so, articulating and striving for an ambitious range of outcomes for classroom literacy education is crucial if we truly mean to give students from all class backgrounds a real opportunity to succeed at the next level, whatever that may be for them. In "Increasing Expectations for Student Effort," Maitland and Schilling (1999) remind us how "merely stating an expectation results in enhanced performance, that higher expectations result in higher performance, and that persons with high expectations perform at a higher level than those with low expectations, even though their measured abilities are equal" (p. 5).

Developing Intrinsic Values for Reading and Writing

Teachers need to develop a repertoire of strategies for piquing in students the intellectual curiosity that will inspire them to care enough to work hard at learning. We need to show students that motivation for reading and writing can be intrinsically rewarding, connected to more than their goal of pleasing their parents or getting a good grade, a diploma, and a job. Creating intrinsic motivation is an art that teachers struggle with daily, and little of what we have to say about how to create or allow for intrinsic motivation is new. Nothing we suggest works in isolation. Similar to directing a play or an elaborate musical, there are many elements, each one needing the other for the whole to be complete: the orchestra, the voices of the singers, the individual parts, costumes, make-up, set pieces and design, the lights, the movement of the actors and dancers across the stage. All these elements we can work on individually, but they must come together in a way that conveys commitment to ongoing dialog and inquiry.

If we see teaching writing as an art, then, like the director of each nightly performance of a Broadway hit that's on a six-month run, we must keep the teaching and learning of writing fresh, inspiring, and attuned to our audience (our students). The audience alone can change all the other parts of a musical, reacting to parts differently on any given night. We have to be open to these changes and the process of learning evolving in front of our eyes. It is a living, changing process that stops for nothing and no one, just as one year we decide *Julius Caesar* is about Power and Control, and the next year, with a different class, the story is more importantly about Betrayal and Loss.

At Durango High School in Las Vegas, Nevada, teachers create environments that model their own intrinsic values for reading and writing. Gary, in his fifteenth year of teaching, sets his room up like a stage. He uses black, gray, and purple shades for background on the wall so he can set up the dramatic black-and-white photos of his favorite authors and poets—James Joyce, Zora Neale Hurston, Ernest Hemingway, Ezra Pound, Emily Dickinson, Walt Whitman, Henry David Thoreau, Shakespeare, the Beat Poets. The entire room is covered with photos and quotes from these authors. He goes so far as to drape a thick curtain across the back where students give presentations and where he stands to read from *Hamlet* and the other literary works he covers during the term.

Meghan, a second year teacher at Durango, has her students display their best poems around the room accompanied by bios and photos about themselves. During the day she invites other classes in for refreshments and to hear her students read their sonnets. After these readings, the students from the other classes can be heard commenting, "I didn't know Judi's brother wrote poetry," and the teachers from the other rooms can be heard saying, "I didn't know Judi could read, let alone write a poem."

Both Meghan and Gary participate in the assignments they give to their classes. And both teachers read their own writing and the writing of other authors.

If we are to help students understand the intrinsic value of reading and writing, then students need to stop the "game playing" in which they each engage. Even the most admirable list of outcomes can be turned into a kind of game, an adaptation of the "banking" concept of education (Freire, 1993). For students, the outcomes offer up a language to talk about what they have learned; whether or not they can put it into meaningful practice is another matter. In Hannah Ashley's (2001) recent account in *Research in the Teaching of English,* proficient working-class student writers successfully "play the game" in their English classes. They earn good grades and parental approval by using teachers' language and applying basic essay writing skills they learned in junior high or early in high school. Yet the price they pay for "giving the teachers what they want" is a suppression of self. And later in college, at some point, the game no longer works when "adjectives [are no longer] good enough to substantiate a good paper . . . Teachers weren't there anymore to applaud you if you were writing" (2001, p. 510).

One of Diane's AP English students suggested that teachers are often unknowingly complicit in a parallel sort of game playing. For too many teachers, the time, energy, and risk required to ensure that learning is internalized (goes beyond rote knowledge) makes "game playing" an unspoken way of dealing with the overload of too many papers to grade, lessons to prepare, individual students to work with. According to one student, "I think with writing that our teachers don't teach us how to use things like similes and metaphors and alliteration—they teach us what it is but not how to use it. You can identify it if you are reading something, but not put it to use" (Brooks Reeves, class discussion, May 15, 2001).

So how can teachers of writing in high school and first-year college composition convince students, and themselves, that we all have something to gain by quitting the game that for many of us, most of the time, seems to work just fine? When we asked graduates of East High how teachers can communicate high expectations, provoke thinking, and dispense with the game playing, Leah responded by describing her AP English class.

> It was the class we created. It added to the entire learning process. The class became a working force and support for all. The timed writings daily and the in depth discussions, sometimes arguments that stayed with me. The writings you had us do were the best. I hated them at first. By the end of the year, I looked forward to the challenge. You gave us a hard question, and you said write about it now, you have fifteen minutes. I thought you were crazy. Before that class, I only had to summarize or explain something. They were tasks disconnected to anything that made sense to me or anyone else in the class. The other great thing we did was we read our writings in class after we wrote them. You made every single student read and we became accustomed to that format. It became a habit, and I learned so much as we discussed each person's response to the question or quote from literary criticism. You made us

do that the first day we came into your class. Do you remember that? The whole class was ready to drop AP. The discussion of the diction, syntax, the verbs and modifiers—looking closely at what tools the writer used was new to me. I came away with a new vocabulary. And learning about rhetoric. About audience, purpose, and context. I quit writing the five-paragraph essay—finally! Writing became real and for a reason. The class was unified and strong. We did have a few battles going though. But, I found out arguments are instructive and important. I used to hate to argue. The whole class posed problems, which set the class on an equal footing. Everyone was trying hard to discover an answer. (personal interview, June 6, 2001)

For Leah, the "outcomes" set up for AP English translated into real learning that helped her make a successful transition to college writing, though not without a lot of hard work. What she learned most about writing in high school was that for all writers—no matter what level of experience, no matter their socioeconomic level or class background—writing is a process that requires revision, discipline, commitment, persistence, and personal investment. Perhaps these habits and characteristics of writers are the most important factors students must learn if they are to succeed in college writing classes.

Notes

1. Csikszentmihalyi (1991) defines flow as the absorbing experience of losing oneself in a task. The experience of flow occurs when a task is neither too easy nor too challenging. Perry (1999) examines how writers achieve flow.

2. Hjortshoij (2001) offers an excellent guide to making the transitions from high school to college writing.

3. The WPA outcomes listed here reflect minor revisions by the Writing Program at UW.

References

Ashley, Hannah. 2001. "Playing the Game: Proficient Working-Class Student Writers' Second Voices. *Research in the Teaching of English* 35: 493–523.

Beech, J. 2001. *Writing as/or Work: Locating the Material(s) of a Working-Class Pedagogy.* Diss. Hattiesburg, MS: The University of Southern Mississippi.

Bean, J. 1996. *Engaging Ideas: The Professors' Guide to Integrating Writing, Critical Thinking, and Active Learning in the Classroom.* San Francisco: Jossey-Bass.

Csikszentmihalyi, M. 1991. *Flow: The Psychology of Optimal Experience.* San Francisco: Harper & Row.

Council of Writing Program Administrators. 2000. *WPA Outcomes Statement for First-Year Composition.* http://www.cas.ilstu.edu/English/Hesse/outcomes.html.

Delpit, Lisa. 1995. *Other People's Children: Cultural Conflict in the Classroom.* New York: The New Press.

Dewey, John. 1938. *Experience and Education.* New York: Macmillan.

Foner, Philip S. 1976. *We, The Other People.* Champaign, IL:University of Illinois Press.

Freire, Paulo. 1999. "The 'Banking' Concept of Education." In *Ways of Reading: An Anthology for Writers,* edited by David Bartholomae and Anthony Petrosky, pp. 348–59. Boston and New York: Bedford/St. Martins.

Heathcott, Joseph. 1999. "Teaching Critical Analysis and Writing to Working-Class Students." In *Teaching Working Class,* edited by Sherry Lee Linkon, pp. 106–22. Amherst: University of Massachusetts Press.

Hjortshoij, Keith. *The Transition To College Writing.* Boston: Bedford/St Martin's Press, 2001.

Jones, Le Alan and Lloyd Newman with David Isay, 1998. *Our America: Life and Death on the South Side of Chicago.* New York: Washington Square Press.

Maitland, K., and K. L. Schilling. May-June 1999. "Increasing Expectations for Student Effort." *About Campus* 4–10.

Mutnich, Deborah. 1996. Writing in or Alien World, Portsmouth, NH: Boynton/Cook Publishers.

Perl, Sondra. 1980. "Understanding Composing." *College Composition and Communication* 31: 363–9.

Perry, S. 1999. *Writing in Flow: Keys to Enhanced Creativity.* Place: Writers Digest Books.

U.S. Department of Education, Office of Educational Research and Improvement. *Realizing the Potential: Improving Postsecondary Teaching, Learning, and Assessment.* University Park, PA: The National Center on Postsecondary Teaching, Learning, and Assessment, 1995.

Wallenstein, N. 1987. "Problem-Posing Education: Freire's Method for Transformation." In *Freire for the Classroom: Sourcebook for Liberatory Teaching,* edited by Ira Shor, pp. 33–44. Portsmouth, NH: Boynton-Cook.

Will, George. January, 7, 2001. "When Intact Families Are Left Behind." *Washington Post* Writers' Group.

6

Making Maps

Helping Students Become Active Readers

Judith Burdan

I am Eratosthenes' heir—the librarian
who measured earth. He took an obelisk,
a well, the sun, and made a triangle:
geometry, simple and accurate.

A cartographer of sorts—I measure
earth with words. I have drawn roads
and made them impassable. I have laid
railroad tracks to serve as escape
routes. I have surveyed rivers and
seas by touch and taste. And yet,
I ignore my point of departure
or destination: only know the lands that lie in between.

Growing up under an obelisk's shadow I
heard the story of genocide, of World
War II, read geography, poems,
swallowed them whole and learned—but

this journey never ceases.
Mapmaking is a life-long task.

—Beatriz Badikian,
Mapmaker Revisited

One way to view a student's entrance into college is to see it as a journey into a
new territory. To become successful citizens of this new place they must learn

how to negotiate the terrain of the academy, as well as master the new language represented by academic discourse. When we all move into a new city or town, one of the first things that most of us do is to get our bearings, figure out the "lay of the land." Generally we do that with the help of a map, oftentimes one of those oversized accordion-pleated monsters that we laboriously fold and unfold, poring over it for the sense of direction and perspective that we desire. As we learn to read this map, it becomes useful to us in at least two significant ways: for one, it helps us locate our destination and the various routes that we might take to get there; for another, it gives us a sense of the characteristics of that destination once we have arrived. To understand where we are, we try to visualize the space that we must be able to negotiate through and position ourselves within.

At first, as we depend on this map to help guide our early, tentative forays into a strange landscape, we studiously abide by its major, easily identifiable roadways. We tend not to stray from these oft-traveled highways for fear that we will get lost, enter territory that is beyond our experience and our comprehension. But as we grow more accustomed to this space, and more comfortable with ourselves within this space, we begin to explore. We seek alternate routes, short cuts, and out-of-the-way neighborhoods. We begin, in other words, to make our own maps. We build on our experiences within this new territory, locating ourselves with landmarks that we have chosen for ourselves, devising routes that make sense to us even as they wind through what had before been a nearly incomprehensible maze, developing a way to describe the terrain to ourselves and others. We transform what was previously unknown space into a world both new and reassuringly familiar, and we maneuver with a sense of confidence, thinking of ourselves as "at home."

In many ways, students go through a similar process when they encounter the new intellectual territory of the university. At every stage of their journey they encounter an array of academic texts—everything from essays and poems to textbook chapters and journal articles—on which they must get a perspective and through which they must find a way. At first the journey seems overwhelming, and so students look entirely to those maps provided by their teachers—lectures, discussion questions, study guides, exams. And certainly these maps are helpful, particularly if they are used as destination maps that aid students in making the journey from Point A (introduction of the material) to Point B (exam or paper). But if students are truly to get "the lay of the land" of the university, and if they are truly to feel "at home" within it, they must learn to map the territory for themselves. They must become readers of maps who are also makers of maps.

Active Versus Passive Readers

Reading college-level academic discourse makes demands on students that are often dauntingly unfamiliar and rigorous. The sheer volume, not to mention the complexity, of material that students are expected to take in can be dizzying.

For many, the reading task is made even more forbidding through a misconception of what reading actually entails. Too many believe that reading is a one-way process, an "interaction" during which "the printed page impress[es] its meaning on the reader's mind or the reader extract[s] the meaning embedded in the text" (Rosenblatt, 1995, p. 26). Meaning merely passes between, hence the word interaction, the reader and text. In this exchange, only one side of the interaction is active, while the other remains passive: from one perspective, the reader is a blank page merely awaiting the impress of knowledge; from the other, the text is merely an inert object to be mined by the reader. In either case, students perceive reading almost as intuitive: the reader either "gets" (in both senses of the word) the meaning of a text, or not, without actually participating in its production.

But a better way to view reading is as a "transaction," in which meaning is created through a movement of ideas across the space between reader and text. "The relation between reader and signs on the page proceeds in a to-and-fro spiral, in which each is continually being affected by what the other has contributed" (Rosenblatt, 1995, p. 26). In a transaction, neither reader nor text is a passive object. Instead, both are active creators of meaning. Reading is thus not a passive process in which meaning is received from or found within a text, but a dynamic, dialectical process through which meaning, contingent and plastic, is created by the active relationship between reader and text.

Put simply, reading is a dynamic transaction that requires active participation and metacognition, or thinking about thinking. Certainly, we must get our students to read as often as possible. Even rote practice has its benefits. But what we really want is to see our students recognize themselves as part of the creative process of making meaning through reading. This recognition should, in turn, empower them to map their reading in the sense that they understand the how and why of successful reading strategies and are able consciously to deploy those strategies. True literacy, in Jeff Wilhelm's (1997) words, "is both the willingness and the ability to evoke, conceive of, express, receive, reflect on, share, evaluate, and negotiate meanings" (151). We want our students to be engaged fully by the material that they read in the sense that they can "receive," "reflect on," and "share" its content. But we also want them to engage with reading through learning to "evaluate" and "negotiate" meaning, critical thinking skills that require not only a sense of one's destination (comprehension) but also an understanding of *how* one gets there. One can only negotiate through unfamiliar territory for oneself by actually doing it and keeping a mental record of how one has done it. Likewise, being able to recognize meaning as something to be negotiated, and being able to negotiate that meaning, requires that readers understand that they bring their own ideas, experiences, and skills to the tasks at hand.

All too often, however, students do not understand reading as this kind of dynamic, engaging process. Too many students see reading as a dreary, time-consuming task rather than as a welcome opportunity to stretch their cognitive muscles and broaden their horizons. To succeed within college classrooms, students need to take an active role in deciphering texts and creating meaning with them. They must be able to engage in open-ended, student-centered discussions. This kind of classroom can be disorienting and even disconcerting for many students if they have only experienced a pedagogy that emphasizes "narrowly defined comprehension skills" rather than response and interpretation (Applebee, 1992, p. 9). Many times, early in a semester, I encounter students who are reluctant or unwilling to participate in class. Some wonder why I want to hear their viewpoints and experiences at all, since they so often have a low regard for their own ideas, lives, and abilities. These students generally signal their insecurity by prefacing their remarks with "This is probably wrong, but. . ." or "I know that I'm way off, but. . . ." Many others have simply adopted what could be described as "learned helplessness"—the belief that they simply aren't good at reading and never will be regardless of how much they try (Carr, Mizelle, and Charak, 1998, p. 50). These students, after years of failure and avoidance, tend to see reading as a necessary evil, something important but largely out of their control. They recognize their deficiencies and are generally eager to improve their reading skills, but they have no clear sense of how to do so and feel generally powerless in the face of their inability to comprehend what they read, while they see others experience reading with ease.

Why do some students develop into successful, self-confident readers and others into reluctant, self-defeating ones? Students' attitudes toward reading are deeply influenced by a variety of factors—ability, effort, luck, others, strategy, or task— to which they attribute either their success or failure. These factors can be divided into several categories—internal or external (i.e., innate ability or applied effort), stable or unstable (i.e., manifesting an understandable pattern of successes or failures, or manifesting apparently random results), and controllable or uncontrollable (i.e., influenced, or not, by learned skills) (Carr et al.,1998, pp. 49–50). Students who exhibit "learned helplessness" are those who believe their reading ability is low, stable, and beyond their control. Often these are students who have learned over the years through an accumulation of failures, or occasional successes, to look at reading ability as innate, intuitive, stable, and uncontrollable—someone is either good at it or he's not, once and for all—rather than as the result of a set of skills that can be developed over time. Having no clear sense of why they fail or succeed at reading tasks, they are unsure of themselves in the classroom and avoid any challenges that might lead to failure. They are prone to give up on reading that they find difficult, or to react dismissively to ideas and opinions that they don't fully comprehend, or to refuse even to make an attempt at a reading task that they might fail. In other words, they perceive reading, to use Rosenblatt's (1995) terms, not as a transaction but as an interaction. They believe that they are supposed to "get" something from their reading, and when they don't, they feel betrayed and empty-handed.

So, how do we encourage these reluctant readers to read? And how do we get our students to see themselves as an essential component of a meaning-producing transaction with a text? How do we transform our students from passive to active readers? If our aim as teachers is to engage and empower our students as readers, then we need to put them in control of their reading and the development of their reading skills. To help them gain this control we need to turn unconscious readers into conscious ones, to "de-naturalize" the activity of reading, and thereby encourage students to be attentive to not just *what* they read but also *how* they read. The best way to improve both students' ability and their motivation to read is to encourage within them a metacognitive awareness of how they read and a belief that a strategic application of purposeful skills and knowledge can and will lead to success. Students who link reading ability to skills that can be learned and improved create for themselves a feedback loop of success: "Basic skills training gives students some control over what they read while it provides students with the resources to improve their skill. It is students' awareness of these skills and their understanding that these skills have improved their reading that restores students' confidence in themselves as readers" (Carr et al., 1998, p. 62). In a more figurative sense, we want them to be able to read with the guidance of maps provided by others—teachers, critics, peers—but we also want them to be able to make maps of their own. We need to look at students as mapmakers and at reading as an individual exercise in mapping a text so as to make it comprehensible territory to them as intellectual travelers.

To empower our students as readers, we need to help them develop procedural and conditional knowledge about reading. We need to help them arrive at a deliberately conscious process by which to read and understand a variety of academic texts, both nonliterary and literary, of varying domains and levels of complexity—magazine articles, editorials, essays, textbook chapters, novels, poems, plays, and so on. In the following pages, I suggest some ways in which we can help our students develop an understanding of the skills that they need to become better and more confident readers. I begin with a discussion of reading nonliterary texts, such as essays, textbooks, and professional journal articles. In the next chapter, I discuss reading literature. I have intentionally separated my discussion because I believe that although there are important analogies to be drawn between the domains of nonliterary and literary readings (there are, certainly basic declarative, procedural, and conditional knowledges that are shared by most types of reading), I also believe that there are distinctive qualities of literature that make the reading of literature something quite different from, even resistant to, the kind of reading required of a magazine essay, or a chemistry textbook, or a memo. I hope that by mapping my experience with teaching these various kinds of reading, I can offer guidance that will help others see a new way to negotiate the territory of their own teaching of reading.

Strategies for Actively Reading Nonliterary Texts

At the beginning of my basic reading and study skills courses, I ask my students, usually folks who had a less than distinguished high school career, a series of questions about their reading choices and habits: Do they like to read? What do they like to read? What sorts of things do they find most difficult to read? How do they cope with a text that they find difficult? In these early discussions of reading practices, many say that they generally read only when they need to know something, or when they have some time to kill. They find most college texts difficult to read, and they frequently admit that their primary strategy for getting through difficult material is simply to read it over and over and over until the information sinks in, or to settle for whatever they are able to glean from their exertions. With students such as these, the initial focus of reading instruction should be on *procedural* and *conditional knowledge* rather than on any specific content. A teacher's selection of materials, covering current events and issues, as well as general interest information, should be designed to engage students without distracting them from learning about *strategies* for reading.

To help students acquire conditional knowledge, they need to become aware of the different purposes for reading. That is, they need to understand that all readers, whether consciously or not, have a specific aim, be it information seeking, or time killing, or pleasure seeking, for every text they read. That purpose influences in turn the kinds of reading strategies that a reader deploys. Most students can easily recognize the difference between reading for entertainment and reading for information—in the first instance, the reader, who just wants to fill the time, tends to skim the material without really paying attention to it; in the second, the reader, who wants to put the text to use, reads more carefully. In my classes, I use the example of recipes to make my point. I'm not much of a cook, but I read cookbooks for pleasure; I want simply to enjoy the illustrations and to imagine what the dishes might be like if someone else prepared them and served them to me. At those times I don't pay close attention to exact measurements or procedures. Sometimes, however, I read my cookbooks in order to prepare a dish, and at those times my reading strategies are quite different: I read through the whole recipe carefully in order to take stock of the necessary ingredients and equipment, I make sure that I know all the various techniques required for accomplishing the task (looking up those that I don't), and I copy down the list of ingredients so that I won't forget anything on my next visit to the grocery store. Hence, my purposes for reading inevitably affect both my level of attention and my strategies for reading.

Once students understand that different purposes for reading require different strategies, we can begin to help them learn the strategies that will give them greater confidence and success with reading college-level texts. Many of the following strategies—asking prereading questions, annotating, taking notes, mapping, analyzing morphemes—are familiar. However, we usually tend to teach them as content knowledge. We simply "tell" students to "do" them. The problem is that many students don't know how to do them well. They don't know what a "good" set of notes looks like, or even why it is a good set. My discussion of these strategies follows what I believe are increasing levels of complexity rather than chronology. While I recognize that some strategies naturally occur earlier than others (for example, one must read a text before it can be mapped), I would argue that these strategies are necessarily interdependent and recursive (in much the same way that drafting and revision depend on one another).

Asking Questions

As they begin to learn how to map these texts, students need to learn how to survey the material before them and use meaning cues in titles, headings, etc., to formulate questions that lead them into transactions with texts. Students should generate questions that allow them to speculate about the content of the text and to think about what they believe is the most important information in the text. They should also think about how they need to approach the text. They need to ask themselves, what is this text about? What seems to be its purpose? What is my purpose in reading it? What do I already know about this subject? How might my prior knowledge be influenced by this text? It is only after this self-conscious querying has given them some sense of purpose and direction that students should actually read through the whole text. Following this reading, students should reflect on the questions they considered during the pre-reading phase to examine any miscalculations they may have made, as well as the reading strategies that lead to those miscalculations in order to learn for future readings. By doing so, they are practicing "forward-reaching transfer"—deciding what they have learned from deploying these prereading strategies that will help the next time around. When they encounter the next text, they need to engage in "backward-reaching transfer"—remembering what worked the last time and applying those strategies to the new text.

Examining how they read generally leads students to see the potential misunderstandings that can arise from skipping words they don't know, or using definitions that are familiar to them but inappropriate to the context, or disregarding coordinating and subordinating conjunctions, or in essays reading only the first and last sentences of paragraphs in order to save on time. Once they recognize the mistakes they make as readers, mistakes often produced by a desire to "get through" the text as quickly as possible regardless of how well they understand it, students are in a position to devise for themselves a way of correcting those mistakes. For many, this might involve a simple willingness to stop and reread a sentence or to have a dictionary accessible when they read.

Beyond general reading skills, students need to learn strategies that will allow them to process the broad range of academic information that they will encounter outside the English classroom, such as psychology, history, or biology texts. Again, the underlying principle should be that of surveying and querying texts, and the emphasis should be on metacognition, on teaching students how to know if and when they are asking the "right" sorts of questions about texts. Here again, students need to think about the purposes of texts from different disciplines, as well as their own purposes when reading them. Students should learn to distinguish the types of knowledge presented and the rhetorical strategies deployed by these various texts so that they can learn the kinds of questions to ask. For instance, if they are reading a text in the field of psychology, they might ask questions such as the following: "What kind of knowledge does psychology produce?" "What kinds of 'arguments' does psychology consider valid?" "How does this community of scholars structure arguments?" "What kind of evidence is recognized?" "What sorts of general ideas and supporting details appear?" Similar questions can be asked about any academic discipline—history, biology, or communications.

Annotating Texts

Helping students to ask questions about texts will help them learn how to annotate their texts, another important reading strategy. As students learn to ask questions, they must learn to record their questions and answers on the pages they are reading. However, because most high school students do not own their own books and they have not been permitted to write in them, this skill is often omitted from their repertoire. Writing in a book may be especially troubling for many working-class students whose parents have taught them to think of books as special, valuable objects in and of themselves, and so see writing in books as defacing. These students need to be convinced of the value of underlining and annotating schoolbooks as an important part of the process of studying.

Annotating, because it involves the students' physical involvement with the text (they must put pen or pencil to paper) is a useful way to illustrate that reading is a transaction rather than an interaction. It is also a way of mapping information within a text, of creating "short cuts" to the important ideas within it. It also allows students to map a larger world by indicating how information within a text supports or contradicts, exemplifies or explains information in other works that they have read and in their own prior experiences.

Many students see studying as something done just before an exam and only then. They expect to get from Point A to Point B through the simple process of going over the material just as they encountered it the first time. Annotating is a way of establishing valuable landmarks in unfamiliar territory. As one student recently put it, "Before this class, I would just jump from one paragraph to another without even thinking about it. I figured as long as I read it, I would be OK. Now when I look at a paragraph, I stop after I have read it, and try to focus on the main idea." Students must learn for themselves what specifically to annotate, but we can put them on that path by drawing their attention to the basic questions that we ask of any text—What are the main ideas and what are the supporting details? In a psychology text, the "main idea" might be a comparison of several theories about how the memory operates. What would be the supporting details? Scientists, the studies they performed, and the findings at which they arrived. In a history text, the "main idea" might be a discussion of the causes and effects of the civil rights movement. The supporting details? People, places, events, and dates. Annotating is a major skill in reading literature as well. It allows students to chart character development, patterns of imagery, and strands of thematic significance—the "main ideas," so to speak, of a literary text. As a student in one of my introductory literature classes put it, "I am a compulsive margin writer. I draw arrows, lines, scribble notes, guesses, etc. I find that it helps make me a more active reader. I also find that writing notes to myself while I read helps me link various texts. I might, for example, jot down a note about how one character is reminiscent of another from a different work by the same author, giving me a fuller sense of intention." Annotating also helps make otherwise dauntingly strange territory familiar by requiring students to put the information into their own words. As one student commented, "Having to put things into my own words is really hard, but it really helps me to see whether I understand what's in the book or not. If I can't put something in my own words, then I know what I have to ask questions about."

We need to help students understand the value of annotating. If they cannot write in their books, then we must find other ways. The ubiquity of Post-it notes allows us to teach annotating *and* preserve textbooks—students need merely to make their annotations on the notes rather than in the margins of the book. Each semester, almost every one of my basic skills students has chosen annotating as the best thing that they learn in the course. One student, a night-shift worker at the local steel mill, who came into my class with the kinds of anxieties discussed in Chapter 1, told me, shaking his head wearily, that learning to annotate his texts was the most time-consuming task he had ever done. But then he added that it was also the most valuable (and certainly successful in terms of his high grade in the course) that he had ever learned.

Taking Notes, Making Notecards, and Mapping Texts

Learning how to annotate texts, with its focus on main ideas, supporting details, and relationships to previous experiences and other texts can also help students take better lecture notes. An effective method for helping students learn the art of note taking is to have students engage in a three-step process. Students should record their notes on a paper that is divided into two vertical columns with the right column slightly larger than the left column. As they listen for important ideas, explanations, examples, and so on, they should record their notes on the right side of the page. After the lecture, they should annotate their notes on the left side of the page. Finally, they should summarize their notes on another sheet of paper before they take a test on the material. While this may be a fairly labor-intensive way of teaching note-taking, the method is designed to open students' eyes to the fact that they must not simply transcribe what they are hearing but they must transact with it, shaping it and making it their own.

Another strategy to help students learn to transact with a text is the use of key concept cards, a study tool similar to flash cards for language learning. On one side of these cards, students might write a self-selected important concept from the material—a place, person, event, concept, formula, and so forth. On the reverse side, they might define that concept and provide supporting details (examples, elaboration) for their definition. With the history chapter mentioned earlier, for example, a student might have labeled a card "Freedom Summer." On the back, details such as the following might have been recorded: "occurred in Mississippi in 1964. Was a move, by SNCC, to register black voters and teach blacks something of their cultural heritage. 60,000 voters registered. At least three men lost their lives in the effort. Helped to push through the eventual passage of the Voting Rights Act." By comparing cards and quizzing each other with the cards, students learn the kinds of details that are important for them to know in order to understand the material. Then using forward- and backward-reaching transfer, they can begin to recognize the kinds of information they need to retain for each discipline they study. These cards are useful in a wide variety of academic disciplines, as well as in numerous employment situations. For instance, one of my students, a local police officer and aspiring FBI agent, found key concept cards helpful in keeping track of the criminal cases he was dealing with. Another student used the cards to help him study for his plumber's apprentice exams.

As another step in the reading process, students should be asked to draw a "map" of a text to create a spatial representation of its contents. This helps students recognize the main ideas presented, along with subordinate ideas, illustrations, explanations, and so on. However, unlike an outline or a summary, a map also allows readers to see the connections among the various ideas. It also allows them to see the disconnections—for example, the author's failure to create a logical argument. Further, designing a map encourages students to recognize themselves as creating meaning for themselves from the text, as engaging in a transaction with the text. In this sense, a map is not simply a reiteration of the material but an analysis. We should reinforce this notion—that by mapping they are interpreting a text. Comparing maps allows students to see that the parameters of any text, while broad and flexible—no two maps are going to be exactly alike—are not unlimited, and that readings of it are not unique and unaccountable—certain information appears in most of the maps, and some maps better represent that material.

Analyzing Morphemes

Finally, we should also emphasize vocabulary building by introducing students to the history of English and helping them to understand words as composed of

various meaningful components, or morphemes—prefixes, roots, suffixes—
and to look at the task of comprehending new words as a matter of breaking
those words down into their components. For example, learning that annotate
comes from the root *nota* (mark) and the prefix *ad* (to) gives students a better
concept of what they are doing when they annotate. They can then take that
root and build other words—note, notify, noteworthy, notice. A short list of basic roots, prefixes, and suffixes can become the foundation for a variety of vo-
cabulary-building exercises, both student- and teacher-generated. Working
with words in this way increases students' vocabulary and gives them some
sense of what to do when then encounter a new word (i.e., parse it and see if
any of the parts are familiar). (For a more thorough discussion of vocabulary
building, see *When Kids Can't Read—What Teachers Can Do: A Guide for
Teachers 6–12* by Kylene Beers, Heinemann, 2002.)

Engaging Students

For the most part, students in my reading and study skills classes welcome new
strategies for reading and studying more efficiently (learning to accomplish
more with less work is a big selling point for these courses). The students are
generally good natured and willing to try out whatever I suggest, admitting that
their own reading strategies don't often bring the success that they would like.
This willingness is also generated by a confidence that what they are learning
in their reading classes is going to equip them for other classes and for the
world outside of the academy. Most of my students recognize and appreciate
the fact that their formal, academic reading experiences will be "useful" to
them: the information accumulated and strategies learned can have a direct,
substantive effect on other dimensions of their lives.

While I believe that it is vital that we help students to gain the reading
skills that will give them greater confidence in dealing with academic texts, I
must reluctantly offer a caveat: I am not sure that this "efficiency" model is sufficient to help students to engage fully with their reading. These basic skills
may help students become active readers of the texts put before them, but they
do not necessarily create in students a curiosity that encourages them to seek
out texts whose "usefulness" isn't readily apparent. In other words, students
may become engaged in the means of reading (its process) without becoming
engaged with its ends (the material encountered). A few semesters ago, the students in my study skills class were working through a difficult chapter from a
history textbook, a complex, detailed discussion of the 1960's. They complained about their struggles to get a handle on the material. I reassured them
that the skills that they had learned in class—annotating, mapping, creating
concept cards—would help them organize and remember what seemed like a
morass of details. Then, amidst this discussion of how to "process" history, one
student asked, "Why do we need to learn history at all? The past is done, and
it's pointless to learn about it when the present is complicated enough." Many

of the other students nodded in agreement. They could understand studying math or English—they could actually use those subjects in their everyday lives because everyone needs to be able to communicate and to count. But they couldn't see the place of history.

Students have a tendency to apply this utility litmus test with even greater frequency to nonacademic texts. Late one fall semester, I came to one of my beginning reading classes fresh from reading a fascinating article about a reporter who traveled cross-country with the doctor who performed the autopsy on Albert Einstein and now had the brain in a Tupperware container on the back seat of his car. In his story, the author relates the journey through the sometimes hilarious, sometimes profound encounters that he, the doctor, and the brain had with various folks across the country, as well as their responses to the famous brain sloshing around in formaldehyde. My students listened attentively while I regaled them with the details of the trip and the neurological studies performed on the brain to determine if genius could be traced through physiological distinctions. When I finished, I teased, "If *you* read more, you, too, will learn all sorts of tidbits to make your world a bigger and more interesting place." And, then, in what I realized was an expression of the attitude with which these students viewed reading, one student retorted, "*We* don't need to read such stories because *you* will read them and then let us know about them."

The gap between what I and they believed to be important to read didn't necessarily arise from a lack of interest in knowledge; it could just as easily have come from a lack of interest in the forms of knowledge that the academy values, forms that practical-minded students might view as less than useful (i.e., directly applicable within a definite context). The students in this class were curious and open to new reading strategies, but they were also interested in efficiency and a minimum of what they saw as game playing. In other words, the territory that they were willing to explore and map with me was more narrowly defined, more destination oriented than I might choose. Understandably attracted to the well-paved highways to academic success, they weren't really interested in taking side trips down unfamiliar roads into esoteric landscapes. I would not at all dismiss out of hand a kind of reading that emphasizes the decoding and processing of factual information with the aim of eventually being tested on that material; certainly it comprises much of the reading that students will encounter at the university, and so teaching skills that give students greater facility with it is valuable to them.

But there is a danger in allowing efferent reading to become the most valued mode of academic reading and thereby allowing it to overshadow the other sorts of reading that students might encounter. We should be wary of contributing to the perceived hierarchy between reading for information (i.e., important, useful reading) and reading for pleasure (i.e., frivolous, leisure reading), a hierarchy that is, for career-oriented students, already so deeply ingrained. As the students in my class recognized, I was the one with the spare time to read interesting extracurricular materials. They didn't have that "luxury." While I concede that the unrelenting demands of modern life force us to prioritize how we spend our intellectual energies, I would still argue that we need to be careful of the messages about reading that we send to our students. Reading efferently trains students in a certain goal-driven mindset that is focused on end products and time-saving devices. It trains them to read like "tourists," to take from their reading what they believe that they need—a certain quantity of information, or a photograph, so to speak, that demonstrates that they have "been there and done that"—and then move on.

What we lose, if we emphasize only efferent reading, is an interest in what Rosenblatt (1995) describes as "aesthetic" reading, in which the reader gives attention to the sensations, feelings, and ideas evoked by a work as it is experienced (33). These affective dimensions of reading, the pleasures and pains of a text, are a crucial part of any transaction with a text. Truly active reading demands the involvement of the whole reader, both intellectually and affectively. This became very clear to me in a recent study skills class. In studying the chapter on the 1960s, the class spent time talking about the emotional dimensions of the text—the frustrations and triumphs of the civil rights protestors, the fear generated by the missile crisis. We spent no less time on the declarative, procedural, and conditional knowledge that I wanted them to master. I just worked harder to help my students gain affective knowledge of the material as they made connections between themselves and the chapter we were reading. I felt rewarded for my efforts when one of my students told the class of speaking about the chapter with a friend who had asked what she was studying in school. She said, "When I started to recite what I knew about SNCC and the freedom riders, my friend explained, 'I was on one of those buses. I was there.' Listening to my friend talk, made the chapter come alive, but having read the chapter helped put her story in perspective." Our students need to put themselves into a text if they want to really benefit from their experiences with it. In reading aesthetically, and not simply efferently, they become more than tourists: they become travelers, changed by their transactions with the new territory before them (Clark, 1998). True literacy is "a window into the social world, where it empowers and emancipates the reader, helping us to become social by understanding other perspectives and to develop a personal sense of agency in the world" (Wilhelm, 1997, p. 152).

It is important as we seek to turn our students from passive (or impassive, as the case may be) recipients of knowledge into active readers and makers of maps that we remember the original impetus of mapmaking—exploration. Yes, our goal should be to create students who have the confidence and the skill to chart new territory as they encounter it, but it should also be to create students who have the desire to strike out into new intellectual terrain, who will seek the unknown, the strange, the puzzling, the apparently frivolous. In the words of Beatriz Badikian, "Mapmaking is a life-long task." It is part of a journey that transforms both the territory and the mapmaker. Our task, as teachers, is to train our students for the journey and then inspire them to take it.

References

Applebee, A. 1992. "The Background for Reform." *In Literature Instruction: A Focus on Student Response,* edited by Judith Langer, 1–18. Urbana, IL: National Council of Teachers of English.

Badikian, B. 1999. *Mapmaker Revisited,* 2. Chicago: Gladsome Books.

Carr, M., N. Mizelle, and D. Charak. 1998. "Motivation to Read and Learn from Text." In *Learning from Texts Across Conceptual Domains,* edited by C. Hynd, 45–70. Mahwah, NJ: Erlbaum.

Clark, Gregory. 1998. "Writing as Travel, or Rhetoric on the Road." *College Composition and Communication* 49: 9–23.

Rosenblatt, L. 1995. *Literature as Exploration, 5th ed.* New York: Modern Language Association of America.

Wilhelm, J. 1997. *You Gotta BE the Book: Teaching Engaged and Reflective Reading with Adolescents.* New York: Teachers College Press.

7

Walking with Light

Helping Students Participate in the Literary Dialog

Judith Burdan

In many ways, literature, as an academic subject, is the most intimidating, the most foreign of intellectually foreign territories for many students, and one seemingly littered with the mines of intellectual game playing. In one sense, the literature classroom is deceptively familiar and mundane—studying literature involves chatting about books, and most people have some experiences or opinions to offer. In another sense, however, the literature classroom is frustratingly unfamiliar and esoteric—studying literature involves analyzing it (reading meaning into something, or taking something that seems to be simple and making it complicated). Many students perceive analysis as primarily a means of tripping people up, forcing them to reveal their ignorance. In an English literature survey course that I taught one recent summer, there was a relatively high proportion of English majors, which increased the discomfort level of some of the other students. One nonmajor, a theology student, included the phrase "not an English major" after his name on his exams and papers as a preemptive strike to remind me that I ought to evaluate the interpretive abilities of this untrained "foreigner" differently from those of the rest of the students. He just "knew" that his reading strategies would not be acceptable in my English classroom.

The study of literature also seems foreign to those students who perceive school and reading as a means to a job. A retired mill worker, one of my neighbors, asked how I had spent my summer. When I replied that I had taught a course on British literature, he was puzzled. "Why would you want to do that? Did you have many students in your class?" he asked. He could understand why someone might need an American literature course, but he could see no reason for a British literature course.

His was typical of the responses I often get from my students. Why take so much time and effort to read literature (and foreign literature at that), particularly when our information culture provides us with ready access via an array of electronic media to so much more, and to more current and relevant information and entertainment? Cunningham (1998) observes that what "is most striking about the changing nature of modern reading material is how it moves us insistently back to a more and more simplistic, merely instrumental reading position. . . . It is one of the great ironies of our time that as the means of writing production get more and more sophisticated, modern reading-content gets more and more playschool" (10). In an electronic culture dominated by the desire to produce and consume tremendous volumes of information quickly, we often reduce that information to sound-bite e-mails, icon-based interactions, and graphics-driven Web pages. Cunningham argues that modern reading is driving out aesthetic reading, what he calls "classic reading," which is solitary, contemplative, and self-reflective. "Classic reading," he asserts, is vital because it "inducts you into personal and moral growth and seriousness, as well as merely informs you of things" (12). Reading literature forces us to slow down and imaginatively, creatively reflect upon ideas, images, and experiences in a way that no interaction with an electronic medium ever can. In effect, we must continue to read literature because it might just save us from our own notions of progress and preserve an essential part of ourselves, our humanity. "Books are not about literacy, or data storage and retrieval," Bolton (1998) insists. "They are much more important than that; they are about life and death" (5).

Why do so many students feel so out of place in a literature classroom? Why do even confident readers feel that the reading strategies that serve them well in other classes will fail them in their literature class? In my experience, students' unease arises in great measure from their uncertain expectations of the kind of learning that happens in a literature classroom. Many students are unsure that they are able to perform the kind of reading required. Nor do they think of this kind of reading as a set of skills that they can acquire. Like my "not an English major," they feel that people are either "good at" literature or they're not.

Students appear reluctant to go beyond the surface of the text because they doubt their authority to speak of the meaning of literature (beyond its emotional impact on them), and so they resist doing so. They see the classroom as territory with a clearly demarcated enclave of expertise, a special place where it is perilous for the uninitiated to wander. Because they do not believe that they have yet "earned the right to speak" in their literature classes, most see themselves as observers of, and not participants in, "the construction of knowledge" (Penrose and Geisler, 1994, p. 506). Students see themselves as reading primarily to discover what an author is saying, or what they believe the teacher understands the author is saying. Their desire is to comprehend the "truth" of what they are reading, and for many the "truth" lies either in the surface "facts" of a text—what an author is saying—or in the "hidden meanings" that only the instructor is qualified to decipher. From either perspective, they don't believe they have much to contribute to a meaningful transaction with the text.

For these reasons, it is increasingly essential that we foster our students' engagement with literature. The stakes are higher than we might suspect in our classrooms, and we need to consider carefully how we go about teaching. We need to help our students to see literature as a world that invites them in intellectually as well as emotionally. As English teachers, "we teach knowledge *about* and knowledge *of*. Knowledge *about* is the data, more or less, of our discipline, and knowledge *of* is something like our spiritual vision, leading in the direction of wisdom" (Heller, 2000, p. 21). We need to help our students confidently bring together the skills of efferent reading (knowledge about) and those of aesthetic reading (knowledge of) in a fully dynamic transaction with literature (Rosenblatt, 1995).

Learning to Construct Meaning

How do we show our students that the literature classroom is a world in which pleasure and analysis can co-exist and actually enhance one another? I believe that we can do so by getting them to see themselves as part of the process of constructing meaning with a text, or by seeing reading as a transaction, as Rosenblatt (1995) describes it. Further, we can show our students that reading literature is a transaction with particular rules that are tied to the distinctive nature of literary texts, in terms of both content and conventions, so that they can more fully participate with those literary texts in the construction of meaning. Rabinowitz and Smith (1998) recommend that we "authorize" our students as readers in two ways: giving them power, "freeing them from passively accepting their teachers' interpretations," and at the same time limiting the freedom of their uncritical emotional reactions by helping them "develop the conventional knowledge they need to engage intelligently with authors" (xv). In other words, as teachers we should encourage our students to express their responses to and ideas about literature within the context of literary conventions. Our goal should be to help our students see, and then to lessen the gap between the subjective and the objective, between themselves as an actual audience (the reader caught up in the immediate act of reading who willingly suspends disbelief and gives him/herself over to the experience of the text) and the "authorial audience" [the "hypothetical" reader for whom an author writes, the one who is unable to suspend disbelief completely, and who recognizes the text as a construct and has the historical, cultural, and aesthetic knowledge to "get" what the author is trying to say) (Rabinowitz and Smith, 1998, pp. 5–7)]. We should encourage students to see not simply what an author says but also to explore the rhetorical choices—the how and why—that an author makes.

When looked at as rhetorically constructed artifacts, literary texts reveal themselves as substantial and meaningful while at the same time being pliant and permeable. Further, placing the writing and reading of literature within the context of rhetorical strategies gives students a greater understanding of audience, purpose, diction, and so on, and helps them to understand better the construction of meaning. Finally, encouraging students to read creatively helps teachers to relinquish some of the power of interpretation (the irresistible authority of the "right reading") to their students and to recognize for themselves that any reading, whether done with or without professional sanction, is contingent upon textual evidence. Such a move frees both students and teachers to explore new readings and risk new interpretations.

As teachers our goal must be to help students acquire the knowledge they need to participate confidently in discussions of the literature they are reading. We need to create classrooms in which students are able to stand outside a text and outside their reading of that text, so they are not trapped within their own subjectivity or kept out by the unapproachable objectivity of the text. We can begin to help them acquire the knowledges they need by introducing them to literary study through the genres with which they are already familiar and through their own writing of these genres. By connecting their writing to their reading of literary works, we can enhance their awareness of the devices in the literature they read and in the rhetorical decisions authors make in these works.

Constructing a Scaffold

I begin each introductory literature class by spending a session or two preparing students for literary study. We discuss what literature is, what its function is within a culture, why it is the subject of academic study. I do my best to serve primarily as a neutral facilitator and secretary as I pose questions and list responses on the board. I ask students to think about what they read— magazines, romance novels, science fiction, or fantasy—and why they read— entertainment, escape, or information—and note their reasons without putting them in a hierarchy. I then ask them why someone chooses to write literary or nonliterary works—to express emotions, to communicate ideas, to persuade readers. We talk about the function of reading in nonacademic situations, moving finally toward a discussion of the academic study of literature and the ways that literature relates to the other reading that they do. I ask students to voice their perceptions of literature, inviting them to draw on their past experiences of reading literature, and again, I try hard not to censure their responses, which range from boredom with or contempt for books that have been forced on them, or good-natured resignation to the irrelevant demands of English classes, to unfeigned enjoyment of the pleasures of literature. I want, finally, for them to see that reading literature is both familiar and different, that it shares many of the functions of nonliterary material but that it is also a specialized use of language with specifically literary aims. An important dimension of our subsequent discussions of individual works as the semester progresses is an exploration of what those "literary aims" might be in those particular instances.

Storytelling

After these opening discussions, I turn to an examination of prose fiction because this genre is the one with which students are most familiar. Storytelling is so culturally widespread that it would seem human beings are hardwired for it. I have used audio recordings of storytellers—Garrison Keillor, Maya Angelou, Jean Shepherd—to let students hear the rhythms of storytelling and to get them thinking about the purposes of storytelling. I have also given students an opening scenario and asked them to write a story from it. Most recently, I gave one class a set of five story elements—a man, a woman, a dog, a diamond, and a gun—and asked them to write a short story using all five elements. I then had them read their stories aloud to their classmates and discuss what led them to the creative decisions that they made. This particular exercise, which produced a large number of tales of love, murder, and intrigue, generated a lively discussion about readers' expectations, as well as writers' choices.

From fiction, I move to drama as another form of storytelling, and again one with which students are familiar in terms of films and television programs. I introduce drama by building on these experiences along with the new knowledge the students gained in their previous reading of short prose fiction. I assign them to work in groups to create a play from one of the short stories we read earlier. To accomplish this they must decide on the set, lighting, costumes, casting, and dialog. They are then expected to explain their choices to the rest of the class and we discuss the outcomes of those choices. In another assignment students must write a paper comparing a movie made from a novel with the original work in an effort to help them recognize the different decisions authors and directors may make in telling the "same" story and to understand the effect of each of these decisions on the story.

Of the three genres that we cover in an introductory literature class, poetry is the one that intimidates my students the most. Once again I rely on the reading/writing connection to build a bridge between the poetry they write and the poetry of such writers as Wordsworth, Eliot, Dickinson, and Heaney. By considering the meters, rhyming schemes, language, syntactic structures, and poetic devices in their own poetic forms, students can begin to learn the vocabulary for entering the literary dialog that centers around Ciardi's question, "How does a poem mean?"

I often introduce the poetry unit through what I refer to as "found poetry." The exercise was generated by an experience that I had in graduate school. One day as I was sitting in my office grading freshman papers, one of my students stopped in. Somewhere along in the conversation he asked why I had chosen to be an English professor. I loved reading books, I told him. After all, who could beat a job where they pay you to read and talk about literature. As he listened to me, he became agitated, jumping up from his seat, and edging toward the door. "I have to show you my favorite poem," he exclaimed excitedly, motioning me to join him. We winded our way through campus, past the library, past the bookstore. I grew curious. Where was this poem? Finally at a street corner on the edge of campus he stopped and pointed to a street sign.

I beamed as he grinned back at me. For a moment we stood there, teacher and student, writer and reader, allied in our enjoyment of the play of language.

I tell this story to my students, and then I hand them a list of words, similar to the one that follows which I took from the front page of the previous day's newspaper.

'Poetry' Found in the Chicago Tribune, 2 October 2000

warlike quality opera lagging godless moral cloudy hugged new millennium bumpy pool waterfall political games rekindle allies suddenly shape international carefully perception white immaculate shadow behavior children family fiery human bite marks oil power green wound spectacular twilight cauldron tableau climbed conceived girlfriend police skirmishes intense shrine fire manned unflappable bungles fears myth dawn view desperate ballet diverted save embryo lethal luck healthy parents want better perpetuate name moment anticipated light ablaze track passed forget guns repeat acknowledges vote embarrassed good arsenal avoided cast smile surge awkward beseeching cut regime strategy food mistake dark deployed sustained soldiers warning peace toll rubber edge threatening sister life worthy arrogance past revelations ingenious grand appeal excess year mind lump inching donor embryo commercial transport money arsenal pivotal

I put the students into groups of three or four and ask them to compose poems from these words. At first, they are intimidated by the activity, cautious about being creative because they fear my evaluation of their abilities. I reassure them that that sort of evaluation will not occur, and encourage them to have fun. As one student in a recent class observed to her groupmates about halfway through the period, "You know, this is just playing with language." Without any further prompting from me, they came up with a wonderful array of poems—everything from free verse, to lyrics, to rhyming verse, to haiku.

Poetry Found in English 231 Fall 2000

Suddenly the shape of fear
shadowed over the spectacular
twilight of the children's anticipation.

While the parents anticipated the moment
of peace, darkness passed.
Through these revelations life
is sustained.
                    —Crystal, Susan, and Phyllis

Human behavior,
a warlike quality,
lagging, godless, morals cloudy.
Parents and children desperate and diverted.
Parents want better
children are fiery
Skirmishes, embarrassed, arrogance and threatening
marks dark wounds lethal.
                    —Katie, Laura, and Jonnie

A New Beginning

The intense fire of the new dawn climbs
strategically over the twilight rekindling life
and casting its smile over the worthy, carefully
hugging the wounds passed on. And for a moment,
peace.
                    —Shannon, Traci, and Dave

Bite Marks

Her fiery twilight
hugged an anticipated dawn
with her excess fears
threatening an anticipated revelation
And with her godless shadow
wounding a spectacular peace
threatened her lover's dark and intense smile
An awkward ballet
sustained by light
A moment; a grand excess
Conceived her shrine of fire
an immaculate myth
                    —Chris, John, and Andrew

Opera Desperately Climbing through Warning

The spectacular dawn's view was
ablaze with cloudy fire. The
green luck hugged like a shadow.
Children smile casting white into
the waterfall pool. It perpetuates
the intense arsenal of ingenious
revelations anticipated by the
manned children. Arrogance mistakes
smiles casting through children,

years, then embryo. Threatens
warlike fiery human bite marks
that shape police and guns.
Dark fears ablaze the intense
shrine of fire. Past revelations
of soldiers rekindle the
shadow of godlessness. The
peaceful twilight climbed intensely
anticipating the light.
            —Mary, Lauryn, and Lana

Want

He carefully passed the rubber, casting a smile on
his girlfriend's life.
Deployed, intense, fiery, unflappable, healthy, arrogance
pivotal. . . .
LAGGing, inching, lump,. . . . . embarrassed.
PARENTS!!
view, children,
threatening, warlike, lethal
Awkward
                    —Todd, Jesse, and Cosmo

I collect the poems and type them up for the next class, when I have the students read their poems aloud and talk about what's going on in them. We discuss the relationship between form and meaning, and we talk about the choices that they made as they were writing their poems. This exercise, like the others that I've described, gives students the chance to do two important things: write their own texts (and to experience the pleasures of doing so) and operate metacognitively as they think about what they have done while they were writing. Having students examine their own choices provides a foundation for their examination of the choices made by the professional poets that they read. Creativity and analysis thus combine to enhance the experience of both.

As students gain confidence as readers, acquire a vocabulary with which to discuss literature, and develop greater facility in analyzing literary texts, I pose more challenging assignments. In an English novel class, I ask my students to write a dialog between two of the authors they have read. Their task is to assume the voices of these authors and discuss a particular issue (prompted by a list I've provided them) with which both authors have dealt or a particular rhetorical strategy that both authors have used. Students have composed dialogs between Jane Austen and Virginia Woolf on their representations of marriage; between Charles Dickens and Evelyn Waugh on their representations of "gentlemen"; and between Dickens and Woolf on their use of doppelgangers, or shadow characters. When I first gave students the assignment, they balked. They argued they couldn't possibly speak for these authors or even know what they had to say on a subject. They complained that I had given them a task that was simply beyond their critical or imaginative abilities. But the assignment stood, and when they turned in their completed papers, they had gained confidence in their ability to "stretch" to meet the challenge. The following excerpt from one of the dialogs, "In Search of England," involves three people riding on a train in England: a tourist, and, as we discover at the end of the story, Jane Austen and Evelyn Waugh. The tourist is getting advice on where to go to see the "real" England.

Lady: Then you must go and see Pemberley. You have not seen England unless you have seen Pemberley.

Tourist: Pemberley? Sounds familiar.

Lady: It is the estate from a novel I—know very well.

Tourist (eagerly): Wait a minute, isn't that from *Pride and Prejudice*?

Lady: Yes, exactly.

Tourist: Of course! That is one of my favorite novels.

Gentleman (mumbling behind his paper): *Pride and Prejudice,* pah. Pemberley—who wants to see Pemberley? If she really wants to see what England has come to, she should go to Hetton.

Lady (sounding slightly offended): I beg your pardon, did you say something?

Tourist: Hetton? What is that?

Gentleman (lowers his paper and looks at the two women): Hetton is a house from another novel you should read, *A Handful of Dust.* There you can see the real England.

Tourist: I remember, I had to read that book in college. But honestly, I did not like it too much. It seems so negative; life does not seem to make any sense there.

Gentleman: That's it exactly, Miss. Life does not make any sense, things don't always work out perfectly so that the right, eligible boy gets the appropriate girl and everybody is happy. Life is not a romance-novel; life is absurd. (He puts his paper back up.)

Lady: How impertinent! Well, as I said, you ought to visit Pemberley. There you will see the true English way of life, just as it is described in novels like *Pride and Prejudice.*

Tourist: I would love that. I really like books like that, where the characters are so lively and one just knows that all will work out in the end. It may not be completely realistic, but it is comforting. It gives the reader a sense of order.

Lady (nods): Exactly. That is why. . .

Gentleman (puts his paper down again): Order? Nonsense! Books like that fool the reader by pretending that there is an ideal world somewhere, when in truth it is all chaos. Such a view is naïve and remote from reality. It is a world for dreamers and escapists.

Lady (sharply): I absolutely disagree, Sir. The world, or society in that sense, can be in order as long as people know where they stand and what their position in life is. It is in books like *A Handful of Dust* where things get out of balance, because the characters have lost their sense of tradition and propriety.

Gentleman (ironically): Tradition, or course! (He folds up his newspaper.) People hide behind traditions and social conventions, so they don't have to see how empty and meaningless their lives actually are.

Lady (shakes her head): That may be true for your life, but mine is quite meaningful.

The students in this class told me that they had to really think about all sorts of details that they might not otherwise have considered. One student was concerned with the setting for his dialog. He wanted it to be both realistic and symbolic. Another was concerned with the diction and syntax that would work for each author. Others thought about how they might best crystallize the ideas that they had gleaned from their readings of the novels. As authors, themselves, they had the liberty to create characters, but those characters had to be consistent with the literature that they had read. Creativity and analysis were dependent upon each other. These students were so pleased with the results of their endeavors that they requested copies of each other's dialogs.

As students learn to think as both readers and writers, to think about the rhetorical decisions that an author makes and about the effect of those decisions on them as readers, they become more perceptive and more confident as readers. They increasingly acknowledge themselves as part of the process of creating meaning through language, even the specialized language of literature. They even learn to enjoy themselves as they . . .

References

Bolton, Eric. 1998. "Introduction." In *Literacy Is Not Enough: Essays on the Importance of Reading,* edited by B. Cox, 1–5. Manchester, England: Manchester UP.

Cunningham, Valentine. 1998. "Reading Now and Then." In *Literacy Is Not Enough: Essays on the Importance of Reading,* edited by B. Cox, 9–17. Manchester, England: Manchester UP.

Heller, Mike. 2000. "What Is Essential about the Teaching of Literature." *ADE Bulletin* 125: 20–23.

Penrose, Ann, and Cheryl Geisler. 1994. "Reading and Writing without Authority." *College Composition and Communication* 45: 505–20.

Rabinowitz, Peter, and Michael Smith. 1998. *Authorizing Readers: Resistance and Respect in the Teaching of Literature.* New York: Teachers College Press.

Rosenblatt, Louise. 1995. *Literature as Exploration,* 5th ed. New York: Modern Language Association of America.

8

A Metalinguistic Approach

Helping Students Acquire the Language of the Academy

Julie Hagemann

"Before letters seemed like little puppets. Today they say something
to me, and I can make them talk."

—Dario Salas, in "The Adult
Literacy Process as Cultural
Action for Freedom"
by Paulo Freire

In the academy we draw on the full range of English—from informal to formal,
from vernacular to Standard American English (SAE)—in the process of doing
our work, but the products of our work are generally expressed in Academic
English (AE), which is based on formal, written Standard American English.
Thus, SAE is the language students most often must employ and the language
by which they'll most often be judged. In most college courses, students are
graded solely on their written products—exams and papers—and more often
than not, the grade reflects not only their grasp of the content but also their use
of language. Therefore, all students need to learn the conventions and language
of academic discourse. For those students who come from homes in which
Standard American English is spoken and whose parents are professionals, the
acquisition of academic discourse comes fairly easily. But for those students
who come from homes in which SAE is not the primary dialect or for those
who come from homes in which a language other than English is spoken, the
acquisition of academic discourse can be daunting.

The basic writing classes that I teach at Purdue University Calumet (PUC)
focus on helping these latter students learn the language and conventions that
characterize formal academic writing. Although this chapter concentrates on

vernacular dialect speakers and English Language learners, the problems and corresponding solutions related to learning the language and conventions of the academy are relevant for all students.

Linguistic Features of Basic Writers

Many of those students enrolled in basic writing courses have not only had little practice in speaking or writing Academic English, but as "language minority students"—students whose home language is not English—(Baugh, 1998), they have still not mastered SAE. These students are both native and nonnative English speakers and they manifest a variety of language backgrounds. Some are monolingual native speakers who use an English vernacular dialect, while others are bilingual speakers of vernacular English and their heritage language. Some of these bilingual students were born in the United States, but they were raised in homes in which their parents spoke the language of the country from which they emigrated. Still others immigrated here from a variety of countries around the world. Some of these latter students come to America when they are very young; others arrive just before attending college.

Native Speakers

Three students, Adam, Tameka, and Bobby, who were in one of my recent classes, are representative of the kinds of native speakers enrolled in college basic writing courses. Generally speaking, the vernacular dialects of English that these students speak are characterized by grammatical features that differ from those considered standard, that is, double negation, *I didn't do nothing,* regularization of irregular *verbs, I knowed he could do it,* and the use of the objective form in a subjective position, *me and my brothers are going swimming.* These vernacular features are not considered appropriate in academic contexts and stigmatize those students who use them.

Adam, a burly student from a rural area, spoke the dialect of Southern Indiana. A football star at his high school, he had hoped to play at the college level, but those dreams were shattered when his SAT scores weren't high enough for a scholarship. Adam is uncomfortable participating in a college classroom—unless he's talking about his family's love of football. "Me and my brothers all played," he told me proudly, "and my dad seen every game. He never missed a one." Writing comes hard to Adam but he is good at storytelling, so I suggested he try to think of writing as storytelling on paper. This seemed to work for him.

Another native speaker, Tameka, who comes from an urban, industrial part of the region, can write an effective essay in Standard American English, but she needs time, because she writes her ideas first in AAVE (African-American Vernacular English) and then translates them into Standard English. She's probably the most sociolinguistically savvy student I've ever taught. Her speech has the rhythm, intonation, and features of AAVE, the language, she says, "we speak, you know, at home, in our community." But she also knows that even though AAVE is a legitimate dialect, a different kind of English is expected in school.

Bobby is a native speaker of Chicano Vernacular English (CVE), a dialect of English he learned growing up in a predominately Hispanic neighborhood and in a home in which he heard both Spanish and English. Both of Bobby's parents emigrated from Mexico as teens. They speak mainly English now, but they maintain their Spanish when they communicate with relatives who still live in Mexico. Bobby's speech is known as a contact dialect because it is characterized by the presence of features that are traceable to another language with which he has been in contact (Wolfram and Schilling-Estes, 1998). In this case his speech has the rhythms and intonations of the Spanish language.

Bobby's "dialect" shares some of the same features as that of a Spanish speaker learning English, though he is a native speaker of English and has a native speaker's intuitive sense of the grammatical aspects of his language. Because he does little reading or writing in English, his essays sound very oral, and his punctuation is erratic.

Nonnative Speakers

In addition to native-born English speakers in my basic writing classes, nonnative language learners, who have immigrated here from Mexico, Latin America, Eastern Europe, and Greece, are also enrolled. Some of my students have been here long enough to acquire all but the less familiar idioms of the language; others are just beginning to become comfortable communicating in English.

Elena who also attended the class with Adam, Tameka, and Bobby is one of these latter students. She grew up in Costa Rica, then moved to the States to attend college. Although she mastered basic English sentence patterns, her writing still reflects her native Spanish language. She is what Valdes (1999) refers to as an *incipient bilingual,* someone in the process of becoming bilingual, that is, learning English. The writing of incipient bilinguals is marked by simple syntax, many grammatical and mechanical mistakes, and much transfer from their first language. Because they are struggling with the language, itself, their focus is on producing it rather than on the rhetorical features involved in an assignment. They may be able to write only a limited amount on a topic, and they may be unable to pay much attention to their audience (Valdes, 1999).

Unlike Elena, Daniel, another nonnative student in my class, is a *functional bilingual.* Functional bilinguals have learned English sufficiently to be fairly fluent in it, but they continue to use "non-native-like" features in their speaking and writing, because they have not yet learned English "perfectly" (Valdes, 1992). They may spell words as they pronounce them—with an accent. Furthermore, their writing may not be organized the way that American readers expect, and their idiomatic expressions may be " off," so readers have a sense that something doesn't "sound quite right" even if they can't identify it. These features occur because bilinguals often learn much of their English orally—they're "ear learners" (Reid, 1998)—and may not have had much practice in English spelling and punctuation.

Daniel emigrated from Poland in his early teens, so he had several years to learn English before coming to college. He knows all the pop cultural references of a native-born teenager, and his oral English is fluent, though slightly accented. His writing, however, is that of a nonnative student. As an "ear" writer, Danny writes what he hears in his head. For example, in a first draft of one of his papers, Daniel wrote "Sands I was a little boy, I always dream to be good in karates. . ."

In some cases, as it was in Daniel's case, it is fairly easy to recognize the problems a student is having in learning English as a second language. The errors that most often show up on students' papers are those related to articles, prepositions, and idioms; in fact, a lack of articles, misuse of prepositions, and deviations in idioms can serve as red flags indicating the writing of nonnative speakers still learning English, even though their oral language doesn't suggest it. In time students can learn to eradicate these errors. According to Veltman (2000), most ESL students, especially if they are young school-aged children, will become fluent bilinguals within five years of arriving in the United States or if they grow up in a home in which another language is spoken, within five years of starting school. The younger these immigrants are when they arrive in the United States, the more likely and more quickly they are to adopt English as their "primary, preferred language," though they may continue to speak their home language as well.

However, even after five years most bilinguals will still have difficulty with the idioms of the English language, particularly when they're using it in an academic context. Research reported by Hakuta, Bulter, and Witt (2000) indicates that it generally takes four to seven years to develop proficiency in Academic English. Idioms are the most difficult aspect of a language to master and are the markers seen most often in fluent bilingual's papers. Therefore, although bilinguals outgrow ESL programs once they become fluent, they still need help in identifying and mastering the nonnative features they retain as well as understanding the linguistic and rhetorical demands of academic discourse. We need to continue to help them identify and correct their language problems. We also need to help them understand the features of a new discourse.

Learning a Second Discourse

We know much more about the processes that nonnative speakers like Elena and Danny use to learn a second language (i.e., English) than we do about the processes that native vernacular speakers like Adam, Tameka, and Bobby use to learn a second dialect (i.e., Standard English). But recent research in psycholinguistics suggests that the processes overlap in fundamental ways.

Whether students are attempting to acquire a second language or a second dialect, their success in mastering a second depends on their ability to develop a different mental representation for each system. Functional bilinguals and bidialectals are able to use both of their languages fluently because they've sorted the two into separate linguistic subsystems and stored them at least partially in different places in their brain. With separate subsystems, they can draw on whichever language/dialect they want to use (Siegel, 1999). On the other hand incipient bilinguals haven't yet fully developed separate places in the brain for planning and formulating ideas in two different languages/dialects. Rather they have a fully developed area for their native language but only a developing area for the secondary language/dialect they are learning.

Incipient second language and dialect learners use their native language as a guide to learning the linguistic rules of their second discourse (Lightbown & Spada, 1999). Because they're unable to make many judgments about what's appropriate in a given context in the new language, they "borrow" rules and vocabulary from their native language, sometimes consciously, but more often unconsciously. For example, Spanish speakers who have not yet learned the rule for forming a negative in English may use the rule from their native language—the word "no" should precede the verb—to create the negative "I no speak English" in their new language. Even if speakers have learned a rule, they may still use it inappropriately. Chinese speakers who do not differentiate gender in their oral speech may use "he" regardless of the gender of the person they're referring to, or Spanish speakers may ascribe gender to such genderless objects as chairs and windows because all nouns in Spanish have gender.

Borrowing from one subsystem to build a second has both positive and negative aspects. When both features are identical in the two languages, the interlinguistic connection usually has a positive effect on new language acquisition. For example, Spanish speakers often have little trouble learning an academic vocabulary because so many of the words are Latin derivatives and are therefore familiar to them. In fact, they may be more likely to know such words as "inundate" than native speakers who tend to use more common Germanic words, for example, flood. However, when the feature under consideration is different, the connection may result in an inappropriate transfer. For example, Chinese speakers have more difficulty than Spanish speakers in learning the English third-person gender pronouns, "he," "she," and "it," because they have less experience with them. Inappropriate transfers also occur when features are closely related, but not identical. In one paper, Bobby confused "tempo" with "tiempo" when he wrote "the tiempo of the music."

As students gain proficiency in a second language, they no longer need to borrow as much from their first language but rely instead on their knowledge of the second language. More advanced learners make active efforts to create and test out hypotheses about their new language (Lightbown and Spada, 1999). When they accurately apply a principle to the appropriate features, they are one more step toward mastery. However, in the process of learning, they often tend to overgeneralize their applications the way native-speaking children do when they first start to learn to speak English. When second-language learners learn, for example, that the past tense in English is typically marked by adding *ed* to the verb, they tend to apply that rule to all of the new verbs they learn, including such verbs as "eat," "drink," and "go" resulting in "*eated*," "*drinked*," and "*goed*."

Ironically, it may be easier for nonnative speakers than for native speakers to learn Standard English (Wolfram and Schilling-Estes, 1998). For Adam, Tameka, and Bobby the task of sorting and separating their home dialects from the Standard American English dialect is harder because their dialect and the standard one share so much syntactically and semantically, and to a lesser extent, phonologically. (By far, the greatest number of differences among dialects in the United States are differences in pronunciation, which impact writing mainly in terms of spelling.) Students may have a general sense that there's a difference between the dialect they speak at home and the one they're expected to use at school, but they may not notice the specific differences. Moreover, they're less likely to be motivated to make the effort to learn to use Standard English because they can already be understood by English speakers (Wolfram and Schilling-Estes, 1998).

Although it may take years for nonnative bilinguals like Elena and Daniel to develop different subsystems, they're aided by the fact that their two languages differ phonologically, syntactically, and semantically. Because they're more likely to recognize the differences between their home language and English, they have an easier time sorting the two languages into separate systems. Moreover, they're more likely to be motivated to learn because they want and need to be understood by English speakers (Siegel, 1999).

Helping Students Acquire Academic Discourse

In addition to learning the differences in linguistic features between their native language and the new one, students learning a second language/dialect must also learn the differences in rhetorical features, such as organizational patterns, obligations to make arguments explicit, and the use of proverbial wisdom (Connor, 1996; Matalene, 1985; Shen, 1989). These differences often impact a students' written communication as much as differences in grammatical knowledge.

Therefore, what Adam, Tameka, Bobby, Elena, and Daniel need is what all basic writers—indeed, all first-year composition students—need: a curriculum that introduces them to the literacy practices of the academy, including that of academic discourse. Gee (1996) argues that discourses are not only ways of reading and writing accepted by members of specific groups but also "ways of behaving, interacting, valuing, thinking, believing, speaking" (viii). In other words, discourse is not only about products but also about processes, not only about language but also about strategy. Thus, like all students, basic writers need to learn to be critical readers and writers, to state claims they can support persuasively, to deal with conflicting points of view, and to re-present others' ideas in their own texts to achieve their own purposes. And they must learn to communicate these ideas in Academic English. They must become biliterate.

The remainder of this chapter focuses specifically on ways to help students become proficient in academic discourse. One caveat to this section is that most of the instruction discussed here should be conducted in the context of a reading or writing assignment. As we have learned from a wide variety of experts over the last quarter of a century (Atwell, 1998; Calkins, 1994; Doughty and Williams, 1998; Long and Robinson, 1998; Weaver, 1996), the teaching of discourse skills in context is far more effective than that in isolated unrelated exercises.

Metalinguistics

Metalinguistics, a form of metacognition, plays an important part in students' ability to acquire proficiency in a second discourse. Metalinguistics is the intentional monitoring and reflection of one's own methods of processing language (Gombert, 1992). In others words, like metacognition (discussed in Chapter 1), which is thinking about thinking, metalinguistics is thinking about language, about one's own production and comprehension of language. By helping students think about the way they process and comprehend both their native language and their new language, we can help students become proficient in Academic English.

To learn a new linguistic feature or rhetorical feature of a new discourse, students need to engage in a four-step process (Long and Robinson, 1998; Ray, 1999; Siegel 1999).

1. Notice a new feature.

2. Study how the new feature is used by writers or speakers.

3. Compare the feature to a similar familiar feature or to a feature used for a similar familiar purpose.

4. Integrate the new feature into the oral and/or textual repertoire of their new language.

1. Notice a New Feature

The first step is a matter of learning something new, such as how to incorporate sources or punctuate an excerpt from a quotation at the end of a sentence. To some extent, this first step is a matter of awareness. Although students may already be familiar with a feature in their own language, such as incorporating sources into a text, they need to become aware of how this is done in English. Sometimes, however, students are not familiar with a feature and must be introduced to it. Most basic writers, regardless of whether they are English language learners or native English speakers, are uncomfortable with such punctuation marks as semicolons and colons because they don't know how to use them effectively. By pointing these features out in an assigned reading, we can provide a context to help students become aware of their use.

2. Study the Feature's Use

Students need to understand how a new feature is used. This can be accomplished in several ways. One is by examining a text in which it occurs and discussing how and why a writer chooses to use it. By posing such questions as "Why does the writer use a source when she writes?" "What rhetorical effect do quotations have on a piece of writing?" "How does the writer incorporate her sources?" "What phrases does she use?" "How are sentences that begin with 'According to XX. . .' structured differently from sentences that begin with 'XX says. . .' or that end with 'XX stated'"?

3. Compare the Feature

Another way we can help students learn a new feature is by building on their prior knowledge and comparing it to something they already know. With second-language learners we might compare a feature, such as the use of question marks, with the way in which they use that feature in their native language. Thus, Spanish speakers learn that whereas in Spanish a question mark is placed at the beginning as well as at the end of a sentence, in English the question mark is placed only at the end. In teaching the use of sources, we might compare citations in a text to our referencing the sources of gossip when we talk with friends.

4. Integrate the Feature

Finally, students must integrate the new feature into the new subsystem of Academic English they are constructing. Thus, for a mini-writing assignment, they may be asked to write a summary of an article they read and to include at least one quote from the article in a sentence which begins "According to XX."

If we use the method of contrastive linguistics discussed in the third step to help our students acquire Academic English, then it follows that the more we know about students' home dialect or language, the better we are able to help students make comparisons between their native language/dialect and AE. While we cannot be expected to learn the heritage language of every one of our students, we can learn the main features of many of them. (See Coffin and Hall, 1998, for a brief description of six languages.) In addition, there are a large number of books that provide an explanation of American dialects in general (Wolfram and Schilling-Estes, 1998) and such specific dialects as AAVE and to a lesser extent CVE (Finegan, 1994; Rickford, 1999; Wald, 1988). Although it may appear counterproductive to use what many perceive as a "substandard" dialect, such as AAVE or CVE, to learn AE, it has been proven to be an effective method. Siegel (1999) reviewed almost two dozen psycholinguistic and educational studies from the United States and around the world that compared a control group of students who were taught only the standard dialect to an experimental group who used their home dialects in addition to the standard dialect. Siegel found that the experimental group mastered the standard equally well or better than the control group.

I was able to provide Bobby with help in adapting Academic English in two areas—using double negatives and using the objective form of a pronoun as a subject *(us little people don't get nothing)*—because I was aware that Bobby's Chicano dialect used these forms. Once I had pointed out the differences between his dialect and AE, he was able to catch most of the inappropriate forms in his papers when he proofread them.

I especially use contrastive linguistics during the editing phase of writing to help students recognize the difference between what they have written and the appropriate form of Academic English. All of us have difficulty "catching" our grammatical, punctuation, and spelling errors when we proofread. This is due in part because we're using the wrong reading strategy. As Madraso (1993) points out, we tend to use the same critical strategies for proofreading that we use for reading a text for understanding. As we read a text we predict what the next phrase is likely to be and then glance at the phrase only long enough to confirm our predictions. We don't really "see" what's there; we just get the gist and move on. In proofreading, however, we have to focus on each word so that we can "see" whether the forms are correct or erroneous. Bilingual and bidialectal students not only are faced with these proofreading difficulties, but in some cases, they may not even realize that a word should take another spelling or another grammatical form. In these cases, we need to point out to students their errors and to show them the correct forms. As we help students edit their papers, we need to differentiate between those errors students can correct once they are pointed out and those errors they cannot correct because they don't know the appropriate form. For those they can correct themselves, we only need to indicate that an error exists by underlining or circling the incorrect form or placing a check next to it (Haswell, 1983). However, for those they have yet to master, we need either to indicate the correct form or to provide them with a mini-lesson. For example, when Daniel wrote "Sands I was a little boy, I alway dream to be good in karates," I underlined the words "Sands," 'alway,' and 'dream,' knowing he would have difficulty with gerunds and infinitives—it's arbitrary which verb takes which form; native speakers know this intuitively, and learners just have to memorize a list—I wrote "dreamed of being good" over his phrase "dream to be good." Without my direct intervention, telling Daniel the appropriate way to phrase his thought, he would not have learned the idiomatic expression "to dream of" and moved one step closer to mastering gerunds and infinitives. Generally speaking, language minority students want to speak and write AE as if they are native speakers. Sometimes, it is only by providing them with the appropriate form through direct intervention that we can help them succeed in doing so.

Academic Literacy

Basic writing students not only need to learn Academic English but also need to learn what academic discourse involves. I begin the semester by helping students "notice" the differences between high school and college as a step toward understanding how they're expected to read and write in college. Students' first reading assignment is "The Difference between High School and College" from *College Thinking: How To Get the Best Out of College* (Meiland, 1981). I especially like this excerpt because it emphasizes critical thinking and is presented as a comparison. Focusing on the differences between students' prior experiences and learning, Meiland explains that students need to acquire language and literacy skills that are qualitatively different from those they have used.

As a prereading activity I hand out a sheet with two charts, a graphic organizer that allows students to make comparisons (see Figure 8–1). First the students fill out the top chart, brainstorming the ways they have used literacy in the past and defining, in broad terms, the characteristics of family and workplace literacy, that is, audience, genre, degree of formality, etc. They also brainstorm what they know about college from talking to teachers, family members, and friends, and place this information on the far right side of the sheet. Then they read and annotate Meiland's text. In the next class they discuss Meiland's description of college-level literacy and then they fill in the bottom chart. Finally they compare the two lists. As they do so, I ask them to think about strategies they have already learned that they can transfer to college classes. We return to these charts throughout the semester as I continually stress critical thinking, reading, and writing. Periodically I ask the students to write in-class reflective essays about their growing understanding of academic literacy.

My next step is to help my students understand the use of academic discourse and thus to motivate them to learn it. Relying on their prior knowledge and using Bruner's scaffold to help them move from the discourses they already know to the new discourse of the academy, I design a unit around the concept of using different voices in different contexts. The students are asked to write a description of a car accident in which they have been involved for three different audiences: an insurance agent, their grandparents, and a friend. I have them share what they've written, and, as read, I point out that, depending on the audience, they have chosen different words, added/deleted particular details, and used different tones.

In the next step they are asked to examine their choices, beginning with a consideration of their audience.

"Which is the 'best'?" I ask.

Adam, like many others in the class, thought the version for the insurance agent was the best because the words were "in the dictionary."

"Then that means that the one you wrote for your friend is 'wrong,'" I pushed. At first Adam said yes; the insurance agent's version would be considered by most people as the "right way" to talk. But several other students

Notes made from discussion with Adam, Tameka, Bobby, Elena, Daniel, and their classmates.

Writing at Home and On the Job vs. Writing in School

	At Home	**On The Job**	**In School**
Purpose	• communicate • remember • express yourself	• communicate • remember • express yourself	• complete assignments • prove that you've learned the material • practice new concepts • express yourself
Audience	• yourself • family	• yourself • boss • co-workers	• teacher • peers
Form and Features	• informal $\updownarrow$ journal lists letters	• specific • accurate • organized $\updownarrow$ forms to fill in	• complete sentences • neat • correct grammar $\updownarrow$ paragraphs & essays

Meiland's "The Difference Between High School and College"

High School		**College**
formal writing, show you've learned the concepts	=	formal writing, show you've learned the concepts
go by the book, knowledge is presented as finished facts	?	go by theory, knowledge is presented as theory—it's in progress—what we know at this point
memorize information for tests, regurgitate it	?	develop beliefs & opinions, have to support with good reasons, ***HAVE TO THINK***
teacher is authority figure—believe this information because I said so	?	teacher is expert—believe this information because I've convinced you with good reasons, it's OK to question & challenge
students are minors, dependent, parents make decisions	?	students are adults, independent,

Figure 8–1 Charting Academic Literacy: Notes made from a discussion with Adam, Tameka, Bobby, Elena, Daniel, and their classmates.

disagreed. Tameka argued. "If you talk to your friend the same way you talk to the insurance agent, your friend'll be insulted. You have to switch depending on who you're talking to." This led to a discussion of writing for an audience. At the end of the discussion I overtly explained the point I had been leading them to make—"good" or "right" English isn't necessarily standard English, but a version of English appropriate to the audience and context. Sometimes it's appropriate to be formal, sometimes not. Because people find themselves in many different situations, they have need to have many languages, including academic English, at their command.

I then move the discussion to one that lets the students examine their own voices. "Which version allows the "real you" to come out? Which allows you to express your true self?" After some discussion, the students arrive at the conclusion that each is a part of their real self. As Tameka expressed it, "I don't become a different person. I just show a different side of myself." This discovery allows me to point out that we play many roles and project a variety of selves at different times. Learning academic English isn't giving up one's self-identity because it sounds so "deadening" as they have told me, but it's simply adding on another role.

Once students understand what academic discourse involves, they are ready to begin to learn it. The previous chapters in this book provide a broad spectrum of ways to move students beyond this point and help them acquire the skills, strategies, and language they need to become academically literate.

References

Andrews, Larry. 1998. *Language Exploration and Awareness: A Resource Book for teachers,* 2nd ed. Mahwah, NJ: Erlbaum.

Atwell, Nancy. 1998. *In the Middle: New Understandings about Writing, Reading, and Learning.* Portsmouth, NH: Heinemann Boynton/Cook.

Baugh, John. 1998. "Linguistics, Education, and the Law: Educational Reform for African-American Language Minority Students." In *African-American English: Structure, History and Use,* edited by S. Salikoko, John R. Mufwene, Guy Bailey, Rickford, and John Baugh, 282–301. New York: Routledge.

Calkins, Lucy. M. 1994. *The Art of Teaching Writing,* New ed. Portsmouth, NH: Heinemann.

Coffin, Stephanie, and Barbara Hall,. 1998. "A Contrastive Look at the Grammar of Six Languages." In *A Manual for College ESL Writers,* edited by Stephanie Coffin and Barbara Hall. New York: McGraw-Hill/ Primis Custom Publishing.

Connor, Ulla. 1996. *Contrastive Rhetoric: Cross-Cultural Aspects of Second-Language Writing.* New York: Cambridge University Press.

Doughty, Catherine, and Jessica Williams. 1998. "Issues and Terminology." In *Focus on Form in Classroom Second Language Acquisition,* edited by Catherine Doughty and Jessica Williams, 1–11. New York: Cambridge University Press.

Ferris, Dana, and Barrie Roberts. 2000. "Error Feedback in L2 Writing Classes: How Explicit Does It Need To Be?" *Journal of Second Language Writing,* 10: 161–84.

Finegan, Edward. 1994. *Language: Its Structure and Use,* 2nd ed. Fort Worth, TX: Harcourt, Brace.

Friere, Paulo. 1970. "The Adult Literacy Process as Cultural Action for Freedom." *Harvard Educational Review* 40: 205–25.

Gee, James Paul. 1996. *Social Linguistics and Literacies: Ideology in Discourses,* 2nd ed. Bristol, PA: Taylor & Francis.

Gombert, Jean Emile. 1992. *Metalinguistic Development.* Chicago: University of Chicago Press.

Hakuta, Kenji, Yuko Goto Butler, and Daria Witt. 2000. "How Long Does It Take English Learners To Attain Proficiency?" [WWW document]. URL http://www.lmrinet.ucsb.edu.

Haswell, Richard. H. 1983. "Minimal Marking." *College English* 45: 600–4.

Lightbown, Patsy M., and Nina Spada. 1999. *How Languages Are Learned,* rev. ed. Oxford: Oxford University Press.

Long, Michael H., and Peter Robinson. 1998. "Focus on Form: Theory, Research, and Practice." In *Focus on Form in Classroom Second Language Acquisition,* edited by Catherine Doughty and Jessica Williams, 15–41. New York: Cambridge University Press.

Madraso, Jan. 1993. "Proofreading: The Skill We've Neglected To Teach." *English Journal* 82: 32–41.

Matalene, Caroline. 1985. "Contrastive Rhetoric: An American Writing Teacher in China." *College English* 47: 789–808.

Meiland, Jack W. 1981. *College Thinking: How To Get the Best Out of College.* New York: New American Library/Penguin Books.

Ray, Katie Wood. 1999. *Wondrous Words: Writers and Writing in the Elementary Classroom.* Urbana, IL: National Council of Teachers of English.

Reid, Joy M. 1998. " 'Eye' Learners and 'Ear' Learners: Identifying the Language Needs of International Students and U.S. Resident Writers." In *Grammar in the Composition Classroom: Essays on Teaching ESL for College-Bound Students,* edited by Patricia Byrd & Joy M. Reid, 3–17. New York: Heinle & Heinle Publishers.

Rickford, John R. 1999. "Phonological and Grammatical Features of African American Vernacular English." In *African American Vernacular English: Features, Evolution, Educational Implications,* edited by J. R. Rickford, 3–14. Malden, MA: Blackwell Publishers.

Shen, Fan. 1989. "The Classroom and the Wider Culture: Identity as a Key to Learning English Composition" (Staffroom Interchange). *College Composition and Communication* 40: 459–66.

Siegel, Jeff. 1999. "Stigmatized and Standardized Varieties in the Classroom: Interference or Separation? *TESOL Quarterly* 33(4): 701–28.

Valdés, Guadalupe. 1992. "Bilingual Minorities and Language Issues in Writing: Toward Professionwide Responses to a New Challenge." *Written Communication* 9(1): 85–136.

Valdés, Guadalupe. 1999. "Incipient Bilingualism and the Development of English Language Writing Abilities in the Secondary School." In *So Much To Say: Adolescents, Bilingualism and ESL in the Secondary School,* edited by Christian J. Faltis and Paula Wolfe, 138–75. New York: Columbia University Teachers College Press.

Veltman, Calvin. 2000. "The American Linguistic Mosaic: Understanding Language Shift in the United States." In *New Immigrants in the United States,* edited by Sandra Lee McKay and Sau-Ling Cynthia Wong, 58–93. Cambridge: Cambridge University Press.

Wald, Benji. 1988. "The Status of Chicano English as a Dialect of American English." In *Form and Function in Chicano English,* edited by J. Ornstein-Galicia, 14–31. Malabar, FL: Robert E. Krieger Publishing Co.

Weaver, Constance. 1996. *Teaching Grammar in Context.* Portsmouth, NH: Boynton/Cook.

Wolfram, Walt, Carolyn Temple, Adger, and Donna Christian. 1999. *Dialects in Schools and Communities.* Mahwah, NJ: Erlbaum.

Wolfram, Walt, and Natalie Schilling-Estes. 1998. *American English: Dialects and Variation.* Malden, MA: Blackwell.

Acknowledgments

I wish to thank Judith Burdan, Matt Gordon, Mel Wininger, and Bill Macauley for helping me think through earlier versions of this chapter. I especially wish to thank Carolyn Boiarsky for her skillful editing of it.

Epilogue

I like my students this semester. Perhaps it is because of the sabbatical I had during the fall term, and I am seeing them anew. Perhaps too it is the group of students this semester; some groups just come together. Or perhaps it's the depressed economy with the nearby steel mills in Chapter 11 laying off hundreds of local workers. I've been told the university's enrollment always goes up when the economy goes down; the workers who've been laid off fill in their time with our classes. So we get the older, more conscientious students, the ones who don't want to go back to the mills.

Perhaps it is also the new, more challenging environment that I've created. I demand more this year. I still maintain a humane classroom, working with the students, listening to their problems, their successes—with their jobs, their homelife—as I did before, but now I require them to know more, to be more independent. I've expanded the number of skills and strategies I teach. I spend time providing instruction in note taking, annotating, forward- and backward-reaching transfer. I require students to demonstrate their process knowledge through mini-quizzes. As a result students have less time to write their assignments in the writing labs during class; they're expected to work on them outside of class, and I've tightened my requirements so that assignments must be submitted on time and tardiness is not an option. But I've also given the students my home telephone number and e-mail address. They can contact me at any time, and I try to respond as quickly as possible. My final grades take much into account. I don't deduct for lateness or absences that are caused by family problems, illness, or outside jobs, and if a student demonstrates progress through a semester I tend to discount the early, poorer grades.

My students are responding well to this new environment. They're working hard. If they can't make it to class—the flu, a sick child or spouse, a business trip, an emergency project at work—they send their assignments by Internet so they're in on time; they e-mail other members of the class for notes and handouts; they leave a message on my voice mail. They want to learn. So they go off to the library to search for information; they head for the computer labs to write up their findings; they struggle through the readings, not once but several times, aware that the instructor will not review the text but that they will need to apply the information to their assignment; and some, for whom Standard English is not their primary language or dialect, go to the writing center, recognizing their own limitations. They have assumed responsibility for their own learning, just as they have assumed responsibility for their lives and their work.

As the semester comes to an end, there is more time for me to work with them in the computer writing lab. "I've come to see how peer review can be successful," one older nontraditional student writes on a comment for an assignment in a technical writing course. Another brings me a copy of a dissertation abstract about the first Challenger memorandum, while another asks me to look over a proposal he has written for the supervisor at his job. The course has become harder; much of the scaffolding has been removed, but not all.

If we are to truly help our students succeed in college English, and in all courses in the academy, then we need to create a classroom that is both challenging and humane.

Biographies

EDITOR

Carolyn Boiarsky has been associated with the National Writing Project since 1978, first as director of the Georgia State University/Southeast Center for the Teaching of English and most recently as the director of the Purdue University Calumet/Northwest Indiana Writing Project. An Associate Professor in the Department of English at Purdue University Calumet, she teaches in the professional writing program. She is the author of *The Art of Workplace English* (Boynton/Cook, 1997) and has published numerous articles on teaching English in the *English Journal, English Education, Educational Leadership,* and the *Modern Language Journal.* A magazine feature writer, she has published articles in the *New Republic, The Progressive,* and the *Atlanta Constitution* and *Philadelphia Inquirer* Sunday supplement magazines.

Contributors

Kelly Belanger is an Associate Professor in the English Department at the University of Wyoming where she coordinates and teaches courses in the composition and professional writing programs. She coauthored with Linda Strom, *Second Shift: Teaching Writing to Working Adults* (Heinemann, 1999). Her other publications include contributions to *Teaching Working Class* (University of Massachusetts, 2000), *Critical Literacy in Action* (Heinemann, 1999), the *Journal of Basic Writing,* the *Journal of Business Communication, Radical Teacher,* and the *Writing Instructor.*

Judith Burdan is an Assistant Professor in the Department of English at Purdue University Calumet. A specialist in eighteenth century literature, she also teaches freshman composition and developmental reading courses. In addition she has served as the academic advisor to the department's teaching majors. Professor Burdan has published articles on eighteenth century children's literature, Jane Austen, and the teaching of literature.

Stephen Fox teaches at Indiana University/Purdue University Indianapolis (IU/PUI) where he is director of the Indiana Teachers of Writing (ITW) Writing Project. He is co-editor of *Teaching Academic Literacy: The Uses of Teacher-Research in Developing a Writing Program,* and has written about literacy, autobiographies, teaching portfolios, and high school-college connections.

Julie Ann Hagemann is the Director of the Academic Support Center at DeVry University near Chicago. Previously she directed the Basic Writing Program and provided courses in writing and grammar pedagogy to pre-service and practicing teachers at Purdue University Calumet. She has also taught reading, writing and grammar to ESL students at the University of Alabama, Indiana University, and the Institut Teknologi MARA in Sha Alam, Malaysia. The editor of *Teaching Grammar: A Reader and Workbook,* she has written articles for *English Journal* and *English Education.*

Diane Panozzo is a poet/writer and teacher at East High School, Cheyenne, Wyoming, where she teaches AP English, International Baccalaureate Theory of Knowledge, and International Baccalaureate Language A1. While at the University of Montana where she received an MFA, she completed a screenplay, "The Silver Lining," which was a finalist at the Sundance Film Festival in 1992. In 2003 she won the Wyoming Arts Council's Literary Fellowship Award in poetry.